7/02

Scientists of Ancient Greece

Other Books in the History Makers Series:

Scientists of Ancient Greece

By Don Nardo

Lucent Books
P.O. Box 289011, San Diego, CA 92198-9011

Library of Congress Cataloging-in-Publication Data

Nardo, Don, 1947–
    Scientists of Ancient Greece / by Don Nardo.
        p.   cm. — (History makers)
    Includes bibliographical references and index.
    Summary: Discusses the life and work of the seven Greek thinkers
considered to be the first true scientists of the western world. Included
are Democritus, Plato, Aristotle, Theophrastus, Archimedes, Ptolemy,
and Galen.
    ISBN 1-56006-362-9 (lib : alk. paper)
    1. Science, Ancient—Juvenile literature.   2. Science—Greece—
History—Juvenile literature.   [1. Science, Ancient. Science—Greece—
History.]   I. Title. II. Series.
Q124.95.N37   1999
509.2'238—dc21   98-3842
                                                                                                CIP
                                                                                                 AC

CONTENTS

FOREWORD

The literary form most often referred to as "multiple biography" was perfected in the first century A.D. by Plutarch, a perceptive and talented moralist and historian who hailed from the small town of Chaeronea in central Greece. His most famous work, *Parallel Lives*, consists of a long series of biographies of noteworthy ancient Greek and Roman statesmen and military leaders. Frequently, Plutarch compares a famous Greek to a famous Roman, pointing out similarities in personality and achievements. These expertly constructed and very readable tracts provided later historians and others, including playwrights like Shakespeare, with priceless information about prominent ancient personages and also inspired new generations of writers to tackle the multiple biography genre.

The Lucent History Makers series proudly carries on the venerable tradition handed down from Plutarch. Each volume in the series consists of a set of six to eight biographies of important and influential historical figures who were linked together by a common factor. In *Rulers of Ancient Rome*, for example, all the figures were generals, consuls, or emperors of either the Roman Republic or Empire; while the subjects of *Fighters Against American Slavery*, though they lived in different places and times, all shared the same goal, namely the eradication of human servitude. Mindful that politicians and military leaders are not (and never have been) the only people who shape the course of history, the editors of the series have also included representatives from a wide range of endeavors, including scientists, artists, writers, philosophers, religious leaders, and sports figures.

Each book is intended to give a range of figures—some well known, others less known; some who made a great impact on history, others who made only a small impact. For instance, by making Columbus's initial voyage possible, Spain's Queen Isabella I, featured in *Women Leaders of Nations*, helped to open up the New World to exploration and exploitation by the European powers. Unarguably, therefore, she made a major contribution to a series of events that had momentous consequences for the entire world. By contrast, Catherine II, the eighteenth-century Russian queen, and Golda Meir, the modern Israeli prime minister, did not play roles of global impact; however, their policies and actions significantly influenced the historical development of both their own countries and their regional neighbors. Regardless of their relative importance in the greater historical scheme, all of the figures chronicled in the History Makers series made contributions to posterity; and their public achievements, as well as what is known about their private lives, are presented and evaluated in light of the most recent scholarship.

In addition, each volume in the series is documented and substantiated by a wide array of primary and secondary source quotations. The primary source quotes enliven the text by presenting eyewitness views of the times and culture in which each history maker lived; while the secondary source quotes, taken from the works of respected modern scholars, offer expert elaboration and/or critical commentary. Each quote is footnoted, demonstrating to the reader exactly where biographers find their information. The footnotes also provide the reader with the means of conducting additional research. Finally, to further guide and illuminate readers, each volume in the series features photographs, a chronology, two bibliographies, and a comprehensive index.

The History Makers series provides both students engaged in research and more casual readers with informative, enlightening, and entertaining overviews of individuals from a variety of circumstances, professions, and backgrounds. No doubt all of them, whether loved or hated, benevolent or cruel, constructive or destructive, will remain endlessly fascinating to each new generation seeking to identify the forces that shaped their world.

Seven Remarkable Thinkers

A handful of Greek thinkers who lived and worked between the sixth century B.C. and second century A.D. were the world's first true scientists; for among them were the first known humans who attempted to explain the workings of nature in nonreligious, rational, and largely mechanical terms. Fortunately, some of their data and theories were preserved, studied, and passed on by Roman scholars, some of whose own writings survived the disintegration of the ancient Greco-Roman, or classical, world and later influenced budding scientists of the Renaissance and modern era.

Mainly for the sake of simplicity and convenience, modern science historians usually divide the era of the flowering of Greek science into four general periods; and each of these periods is represented in this volume by one or more of the seven remarkable thinkers whose lives and achievements are chronicled herein. The first period, lasting from about 600 to just before 400 B.C., is referred to as the pre-Socratic because it largely predated the important influence of the Athenian philosopher Socrates. One of its most profound and lasting legacies was the formulation of the original atomic theory of matter, introduced by Leucippus, but expanded and perfected by Democritus, a contemporary of Socrates. Although most ancient thinkers did not agree with the idea that all things are composed of tiny individual particles called atoms, the idea survived and eventually helped lay the groundwork of modern chemistry and physics.

The second period of Greek science spanned mainly the fourth century B.C. During these years many schools of philosophic-scientific endeavor, the forerunners of modern universities, were established in Greek cities. The most famous were those founded by Plato (the Academy) and Aristotle (the Lyceum), the two scholars whose ideas and teachings dominated the period. In addition to his numerous important philosophical works, Plato provided an early model of the cosmos that proved highly influential to later thinkers. His most famous pupil, Aristotle, went on to produce an enormous output of theories and writings covering a wide range of subjects, including what later became the scientific disciplines of astronomy, biology, zoology, and physics. Aristotle's friend, Theophrastus, almost single-handedly founded the science of botany in the same period.

The third period of Greek science, called the Hellenistic (meaning "Greek-like"), lasted from about 300 to 100 B.C., during which Greek culture spread over much of the Near East, including Egypt. It was in Egypt's capital, Alexandria, that the greatest of all ancient universities, the Museum, flourished. In this era, the outstanding mathematician and inventor was Archimedes of Syracuse, who as a young man studied at the Museum. In addition to his discovery of the principles governing bodies immersed in liquids, he is famous for his design of innovative and lethal weapons to defend his native city from attack.

The fourth period, usually called the Roman or Greco-Roman era of Greek science, lasted from about 100 B.C. to A.D. 200 (or A.D. 600 if one counts later Greek writers organizing and commenting on the works of the early pioneers). The most important famous scientific thinkers and writers of this period were Galen and Ptolemy. Galen brought the ancient science and practice of medicine to its highest level; and Ptolemy, who worked at the Alexandrian Museum, constructed an astronomical and geographical world view, based largely on models by Aristotle and others, that shaped the thinking of European scholars until as late as the sixteenth century.

In this ancient Greek painting, instructors teach students to read and play music. Some of the more ambitious students became philosophers and scientists.

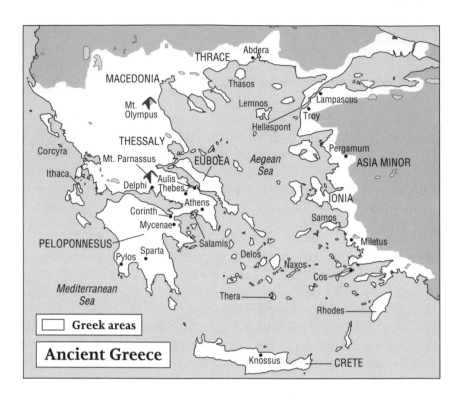

Ancient Greece

Greek areas

Eventually, several of Ptolemy's ideas, like many of those advanced by earlier Greeks, were proved wrong. Indeed, the importance of Democritus, Plato, Aristotle, Theophrastus, Archimedes, Galen, Ptolemy, and their Greek predecessors and colleagues has less to do with their being right or wrong and more to do with the spirit of inquiry that motivated them. By constantly questioning and probing the workings of nature, they set an inspiring example for the modern scientists whose discoveries, in the last three centuries, have transformed and revolutionized human civilization.

CHAPTER 1

A Brief History of Greek Science

Beginning about 600 B.C., the ancient Greeks became the first people in the world to develop a systematic and in some ways almost modern approach to the study of science. The Egyptians and Babylonians had amassed a great deal of scientific observation and data over the course of more than two millennia before the rise of Greek learning. But prior to that auspicious rise, people everywhere, including Greece, attributed natural forces and phenomena, as well as control over human destiny, to various gods, spirits, and other supernatural elements. Because this seemed neatly to explain how the world worked, the kind of scientific questioning, research, and experimentation taken for granted today was almost unheard-of.

Historians George Botsford and Charles Robinson point out,

> With the accumulation of knowledge and the growth of an inquiring spirit . . . [the early Greek scientists] could not satisfy themselves with such reasoning. . . . The contribution of the Greek mind, brilliantly imaginative and untrammeled by religious or other convention, was to pierce beneath the fact to the underlying cause, and thus to create real science.[1]

In seeking the underlying principles of nature, the Greeks largely removed the gods and other supernatural elements from scientific study and discussion. As modern scientists do, they tended to see the heavenly bodies and other facets of nature as material objects obeying natural laws rather than as personalized beings. "It was assumed, for the first time in history," renowned classical scholar Rex Warner explains, "that the investigator was dealing with a universe that was a 'cosmos'—that is to say an orderly system governed by laws which could be discovered by logical thought."[2]

11

"Let It Be in the Light"

This fresh, assertive, independent attitude, characterized by a burning curiosity about how nature works, grew at least in part out of the Greeks' early cultural and political development, which was then unique in the world. By the ninth century B.C., Greece had evolved into a number of small and fiercely independent city-states, each seeing itself as a tiny nation unto itself. As time went on, the independence and individuality that characterized these states came to be reflected in the attitudes and characters of the people themselves. The then novel idea arose that people should not be mere servile puppets doing the bidding of omnipotent monarchs; but rather that each person has worth and dignity and deserves to be free to author his or her own destiny. The Greeks expressed this noble concept in their literature, most notably in their great national epic, the *Iliad*, credited to the ninth- or eighth-century bard Homer, in which the epic events of the legendary Trojan War spring more from the actions of the characters than from the dictates of fate.

Homer, the early Greek poet whose epic poem, the Iliad, *exerted enormous influence over generations of Greek thinkers.*

Some of the *Iliad*'s stirring lines also contain the seeds of that mental quality that most typified the early Greek thinkers—the fervent desire to know the truth of things. "Deliver us from this fog," the hero Ajax prays to Zeus, leader of the gods, "and make the sky clear so that our eyes can see. If we must die, let it be in the light." [3] Indeed, the cry of "let it be in the light" echoed down the corridors of ancient Greek science, a brilliant flame illuminating the otherwise intellectual darkness of Western civilization and pointing the way to the future. In the first period of Greek science, the pre-Socratic, spanning the sixth and fifth centuries B.C., a few generations of Greek truth-seekers inquired into diverse aspects of nature; and in so doing they laid the groundwork for most of the major scientific disciplines, including astronomy, physics, chemistry, biology, and medicine.

These disciplines were at first neither separate from one another nor very distinct and specialized, as they are today. In fact, during this initial period of Greek intellectual endeavor, no clear distinction yet existed between science and philosophy. In modern terms, one might define the distinction between the two fields this way: science involves observation, collecting data, and experimentation, followed by the drawing of provable conclusions about what has been learned; whereas philosophy begins with observations and then proceeds directly to logical and usually general speculations and arguments that need not produce tangible, provable results. Most ancient Greek thinkers mixed these two approaches in varying degrees.

The Search for the *Physis*

This was particularly true of the pre-Socratic Greek scientists, most of whom can be grouped into two schools, or intellectual traditions. The first school was the Ionian, encompassing the Greek city-states clustered along the western coast of Asia Minor (what is now Turkey), an area known in ancient times as Ionia. The first important Ionian thinker, Thales, emerged in the first half of the sixth century B.C. in the region's leading city, Miletus. Already a center of mercantile and colonizing activity and a producer of fine poetry and other literature, Miletus had direct contacts, both commercial and cultural, with older Eastern civilizations. Thales himself, for instance, borrowed some of his mathematical ideas from Egypt and astronomical ones from Babylonia. Thus, Greek science was first nurtured in a cosmopolitan atmosphere rich in ideas from many lands.

Unlike his eastern counterparts, however, Thales attempted to describe how the universe works without resorting to the supernatural or to any other power outside of nature itself. So far as is known, he was the first person to refer to the known universe as the cosmos, which, he reasoned, is ordered, rational, and comprehensible.

Thales of Miletus, the first important figure of the Ionian philosophical-scientific tradition, searched for the underlying causes of natural events.

According to Thales, to understand the cosmos one must search for its *physis* (from which the word "physics" is derived), its nature or underlying physical principle. Because he left no writings, his views come from descriptions in the works of later Greeks. For example, Aristotle stated that Thales

13

held that the earth rests upon water. Probably the idea was suggested to him by the fact that the nutriment of everything contains moisture, and that heat itself is generated out of moisture. . . . He drew his notion also from the fact that the seeds of everything have a moist nature. . . . The earth stays in place, he explained, because it floats like wood or some such substance of nature to let it float upon water but not upon air.[4]

Although we now know that this theory is incorrect, for its time it was bold in that it postulated a material, rather than supernatural, *physis* for the world—in this case various manifestations of water.

Other early Greeks offered alternative ideas about the nature of the *physis*. Thales' best-known pupil, Anaximander (ca. 611 to 547 B.C.), for example, postulated that nature's basic underlying substance was an eternal, unchanging, and invisible substance that he called the "Boundless" or "Unlimited." Through the agency of circular motion, he said, the principal elements that make up everything in the universe—earth, water, air, and fire—had arisen from the Boundless. A ring of fire had burst into existence in the heavens and this large ring had subsequently broken down into several smaller rings, which became the sun, moon, and stars. This concept is remarkably like the modern view of the solar system's formation, in which the burning sun formed first and the planets later coalesced from its leftover materials.

From a modern viewpoint, Anaximander's most extraordinary proposal concerned the origins of life. He held that the first living creatures came into being in water and that in time these creatures crawled onto the dry land and adapted themselves to their new surroundings, concepts accepted by modern biologists. Furthermore, he suggested, human beings developed the same way. According to the second-century A.D. Christian writer Hippolytus of Rome, Anaximander advocated that "man came into being from an animal other than himself, namely the fish, which in early times he resembled."[5] Though lacking much in the way of evidence and explanation, this theory of organic evolution was the direct, albeit distant, forerunner of the one developed in the nineteenth century by English biologist Charles Darwin.[6]

A later Ionian, Anaxagoras, advanced a different explanation of the *physis*, which opened up another line of thinking about the origins of living things. Unlike his predecessors, each of whom had singled out one element as the primary natural substance,

Anaxagoras proposed that manifestations of all elements are present in all things. His thesis grew at least in part from his observations of the act and consequences of eating. He noted that when people eat bread, fruits, and vegetables, they grow flesh, bones, skin, and hair. How could this happen, he wondered, unless the "seeds" of flesh, bones, skin, and hair were present in the food when it was consumed? "For how could hair come from what is not hair, or flesh from what is not flesh?" Thus, he concluded, the tiny seeds of all things must have existed from the beginning of time and "in everything there is a little bit of everything else." Furthermore, he stated, "whatever there is most of in particular things determines their nature . . . for none of the products is ever like any other. And that being so, we must believe that all this variety of things was present in the original whole."[7]

The Ionian thinker Anaxagoras suggested that "in everything there is a little bit of everything else."

The Music of the Heavenly Spheres

The second early Greek philosophical-scientific school was located among the many Greek colonies of southern Italy. About 530 B.C., the philosopher Pythagoras, a resident of the Aegean island of Samos, migrated to the Italian city of Crotona, along with some of his followers. There, they established what later became known as the "Pythagorean" school, dedicated to the study of math, astronomy, music, theology, and other subjects.

Pythagoras and most of his followers differed from the Ionians by choosing numbers as nature's underlying principle, rather than material elements such as water or microscopic seeds. The Pythagoreans at first thought of natural objects as having forms defined by precise geometric shapes and mathematical principles. They viewed the universe as being highly ordered, grand, and noble. The most noble and perfect of the existing geometrical shapes, they held, was the sphere; so they pictured the heavens as consisting of a variety of spheres nesting within one another, a notion that profoundly influenced later Greek thinkers, including Aristotle and Ptolemy. According to the Pythagoreans, the stars, planets, and even the earth are spheres like the sun and moon.[8]

And these are contained within larger spheres. The first holds the stationary earth and its environs; a second and movable one holding the fixed stars and other heavenly bodies encases the first; and a third sphere, looming still farther out, in a realm beyond the view of earthlings, serves as the home of the gods (who merely dwell within rather than control this grand cosmic scheme).

The Pythagoreans also postulated that, because the positions and movements of the heavenly spheres were all part of a single, perfectly tuned mathematical scheme, these bodies must, like the strings of a lyre, produce harmonious musical effects. The third-century A.D. Greek commentator, Alexander of Aphrodisias, summed up the idea this way:

> The Pythagoreans said that the bodies which revolve around the center [of the universe] have their distances in proportion, and some revolve more quickly, others more slowly, the sound which they make during the motion being deep in the case of the slower, and high in the case of the quicker; these sounds then, depending on the ratio of the distances, are such that their combined effect is harmonious.[9]

A later Pythagorean, Philolaus, perhaps a grandson of one of the original founders of the Crotona school, suggested, in very basic terms, what is now known to be the correct view of the cos-

Pythagoras lectures a group of women. He taught that the heavenly bodies produce harmonious musical effects.

mos. He was the first known thinker to reject the geocentric, or earth-centered, cosmos, and to demote the earth to the status of a mere planet. His cosmic model featured several other modern views as well. As the renowned science historian George Sarton summarized it, at the center of Philolaus's universe is the "central fire,"

> which is also the central force or central motor. Around it rotate ten bodies: first the counter-earth, which always accompanies the earth and shades the fire from it, second, the earth itself, then the moon, the sun, and the five planets [Mercury, Venus, Mars, Jupiter, and Saturn; the others had to await the invention of the telescope], and finally the fixed stars. We do not see the counter-earth because the earth is always turning its back to it, that is, to the center of the universe. This implies that the earth rotates around its own axis [once each year], while it turns around the center of the world.[10]

This was a bold and staggering concept for its time, despite some minor errors in its details (the counter-earth and an orbiting rather than central sun). But because the geocentric view was time-honored and universally accepted, and also because Philolaus (like other ancient astronomers) failed to conduct the sophisticated experiments necessary to document his ideas, his cosmic model was rejected or simply got lost in the growing shuffle of conflicting scientific opinions.

Another essentially correct scientific idea that was rejected by most ancient thinkers was introduced in the latter part of the pre-Socratic period, in fact, during Socrates' lifetime, by Leucippus, possibly a native of Miletus. Democritus, a younger contemporary of Socrates, developed Leucippus's ideas about tiny, invisible particles called atoms; but like Philolaus's views, the first atomic theory was too novel and bold a concept to be accepted into the prevailing scientific mainstream. Only because a handful of later Greek and Roman thinkers kept it alive did this profound revelation survive the ages.

Science Gains Its Own Identity

The decades following the death of the Athenian philosopher Socrates in 399 B.C. marked an important turning point in the evolution of ancient science. Some Greek thinkers began to develop a more definite system, or organized approach, to the study of science. Although this new approach was by no means universally

This nineteenth-century painting depicts the philosopher Socrates conversing with the young Alcibiades, who would later become an important and controversial Athenian politician.

accepted and applied, and by modern standards rather rudimentary, it constituted the beginning of science's separation from philosophy and formulation of its own unique identity.

Socrates himself turned out to be instrumental in this early development of a systematic approach to science, which was ironic because he was not a scientist. In fact, he was opposed to the study of nature, advocating that dwelling on the physical, mechanical aspects of things diverted one's attention from what was really important. This, he said, was an understanding of the meaning of such ethical concepts as goodness, wisdom, and justice, and how human beings should best apply them to improve themselves and society. To find the "essences," or underlying truths, of these concepts, he proposed, one had to define them; and to define them, one had to examine them closely under varying circumstances.

Since no systematic method for such examination yet existed, Socrates formulated one, which has since come to be called the Socratic method in his honor. He asked a person a series of thoughtful questions about a subject, all the while professing himself to be ignorant of the answers (which was frequently the case). The respondent's series of answers often became a trail leading to the discovery of the truth of the subject as it related to him or her.

Typically during such cross-examination, the participants would disprove and discard some of the ideas and hypotheses the respondent had suggested. Socrates, Rex Warner explains,

> would take the hypothesis of the person under examination—a conventional definition, say, of courage or of justice—and, by testing it with the aid of examples taken from real life, would prove it to be inadequate or self-contradictory. The process would lead to another hypothesis which would be examined in its turn and, as a rule, also rejected.[11]

By this process of trial and error, the questioner and respondent would eventually arrive at an answer that both agreed approximated the truth. Of course, Socrates' main strategy in using this method was to define goodness and other abstract qualities of the human spirit. However, his pupil Plato, and later Plato's own student, Aristotle, attempted to apply this same logical system of inquiry to the study of natural phenomena. The result was a primitive form of the scientific method.

One of the many fanciful reconstructions of Plato's likeness (his true appearance remains unknown). A student of Socrates, Plato in turn taught Aristotle.

As science steadily gained its own identity separate from that of philosophy, it also began itself to separate into the sub-disciplines, or branches, that are familiar today as astronomy, biology, botany, physics, mechanics, and so on. Among the early pioneers of astronomy and cosmology (the study of the origins and structure of the universe) were Plato and Aristotle. Building on some of the concepts of the pre-Socratics, these two intellectual giants, who dominated Greek science in the fourth century B.C., advanced a version of a static, geocentric universe that became the most widely accepted cosmic model of ancient times.[12] Later, in the second century A.D., the astronomer Ptolemy elaborated and perfected their system, which, later still, medieval scholars enshrined as infallible doctrine.

Aristotle also made huge strides in the fields of biology and zoology, including an ingenious system for classifying animals; and physics as well, in which he made educated guesses about the nature of matter and the motion of material bodies. The emerging field of botany was dominated in this period by Aristotle's colleague and friend, Theophrastus, who produced voluminous writings about nearly all aspects of the plants known in his time.

An Impressive Accumulation of Medical Knowledge

Paralleling and benefiting from the biological studies of Aristotle and Theophrastus were the equally impressive accomplishments of Greek physicians and medical researchers. Greece, like Egypt, produced skilled healers during its earliest centuries. Eventually, highly respected medical schools arose, the two most celebrated being those at Cnidus and Cos, both located just northwest of Rhodes, a large island in southwestern Ionia. Little is known about how these schools operated but scholars agree that they featured clinical researches, classroom lessons, and practical apprenticeship. Students took a solemn oath to help the sick, to love humanity as dearly as their profession, and never to take a life nor sexually abuse a patient.[13]

The Cos school, overseen in the second half of the fifth century by Hippocrates, later called the father of medicine, produced hundreds of writings on such topics as anatomy, surgery, treatment by diet and drugs, diseases of women and children, and medical ethics. The most important contributions of this and the Cnidus school was a major separation of medical theory from religion and philosophy and the firm establishment of medicine as a true scientific discipline. As noted scholar Robert Downs explains:

> The school of medicine represented by Hippocrates had an approach to the art far in advance of anything preceding it and similar in spirit to modern medical theory and practice. There are few traces of superstition and hardly any reference to religion in the Hippocratic writings. His method was to ignore all the gods and to hold instead that disease is a natural phenomenon governed by natural laws.[14]

Hippocrates and his colleagues envisioned illness as resulting from an imbalance of four essential bodily fluids or secretions, called humors (blood, phlegm, yellow bile, and black bile). With only minor variations, this theory of sickness was accepted by most physicians until the eighteenth century. Although finally proven wrong, it was an honest and logical attempt to explain health and illness in strictly physical terms.

In the early third century B.C., during the fruitful Hellenistic period of Greek science (ca. 300–100 B.C.), the focus of new medical research shifted from Cos and other sites in Greece to Alexandria, where Herophilus of Chalcedon, who had trained at Cos, established the Alexandrian medical school. He and his pupil Erasistratus made important strides, especially in anatomy, including descriptions of the motor nerves (which initiate muscular activity) and sensory nerves (which carry messages to the brain); the ovaries and fallopian tubes in the female reproductive tract; and the digestion of food. Some four centuries later, in Greek science's so-called Greco-Roman period (ca. 100 B.C.–A.D. 200), Galen, one of the two greatest of all Greek physicians (along with Hippocrates), became famous for his mastery, application, and often detailed description of the considerable medical knowledge by then accumulated.

The early Greek physician Hippocrates, who later became known as the "father of medicine."

Mechanical Wizards

As they did in astronomy, biology, botany, and medicine, the Greeks laid the foundations for the science of mechanics, a branch of physics dealing with the effects of energy and forces on material bodies and with machines, both simple and complex. As it happens, the fourth-century A.D. Greek mathematician Pappus of Alexandria devoted the eighth book of his large treatise on math to the discipline of mechanics. He provides us with a concise summary of the important mechanical arts of his day:

> 1. The art of the pulley men [meant more broadly as those who conceive and make lifting devices]. . . . With their machines they need only a small force to overcome the natural tendency of large weights and lift them to a height. 2. The art of the makers of the engines of war. . . . They design catapults to fling missiles of stone and iron and the like a considerable distance. 3. The art of contrivers of machines, properly so-called. For example, they build water-lifting machines by which water is more easily raised from a great depth. 4. The art of those who contrive marvelous devices [mechanical clocks, puppets, toys]. . . . 5. The art of the sphere makers. . . . They construct a model of the heavens [miniature planetarium with moving parts powered by a small water wheel].[15]

21

By Pappus's time, all of these mechanical applications had been in general use for centuries. He added nothing new of any significance, being content to list what was already known and to praise the great pioneers of the past. The first important such pioneer was the third-century B.C. scholar Strato (or Straton) of Lampsacus, later known as "the Physicist," who worked first in Athens and later in Alexandria. Like his illustrious predecessor Aristotle,

A modern painting of Archimedes portrays him as a grinning middle-aged man holding a compass and a scientific treatise.

Strato was fascinated by many natural phenomena; but he was especially interested in the concepts of force and motion and how they applied to everyday objects. He disagreed with Aristotle on a number of points, including the existence of atoms and voids. Whereas Aristotle had rejected Democritus's theory of matter, Strato was among the handful of post-Socratic thinkers who endorsed it, saying that it satisfactorily explained how light could pass through water and how heat could flow from body to body.

Strato's immediate successors carried the science of mechanics even further. His younger contemporary, Archimedes, is acknowledged as the greatest inventor of ancient times. In the theoretical realm, Archimedes discovered important mathematical formulas pertaining to the volumes of spheres, cylinders, and other solid figures, as well as the basic principles of floating bodies. In the practical area, he experimented with levers, pulleys, and other simple machines, demonstrating their principles in large-scale and, at the time, astonishing real-life applications, the most famous being devastating weapons of war.

One of Archimedes' own contemporaries, Ctesibius (pronounced t'SIB-ee-us), was also a mechanical wizard. The son of an Alexandrian barber, Ctesibius early showed his aptitude for invention, including the idea for the simple cylinder and plunger, the basis for numerous machines, both ancient and modern (including the cylinders and pistons in automobile engines). One of its greatest applications in ancient times was in water pumps to raise water in mines and to aid in irrigation. The Roman architect Vitruvius left this description of the device:

> It would be of bronze. At the bottom would be twin cylinders, a small distance apart, having pipes converging in the shape of a fork, meeting in a vessel in the middle. In this vessel would be valves, accurately fitted over the upper openings of the pipes, which stop up the openings of the pipes and do not allow that which the air has forced into the vessel to escape. . . . Pistons, smoothly turned and treated with oil [as a lubricant] are inserted into the cylinders from above; and thus confined, they are worked with rods and levers. As the valves close the openings, the air and water in the cylinders will be driven onwards.[16]

Ctesibius and later Greek mechanical scientists, among them his pupil, Philo of Byzantium, and the first-century A.D. inventor Hero (or Heron) of Alexandria, became well known, like Archimedes, for designing large and lethal artillery devices. These included

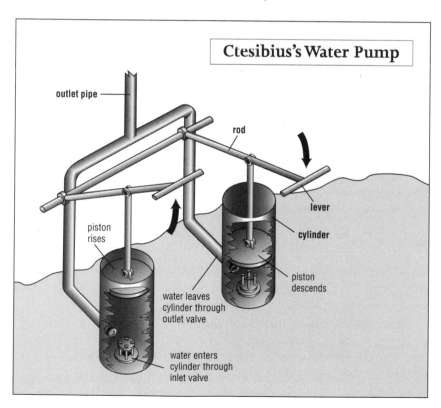

Ctesibius's Water Pump

outlet pipe

rod

lever

piston rises

cylinder

piston descends

water leaves cylinder through outlet valve

water enters cylinder through inlet valve

The Romans use catapults in their siege of Carthage in 146 B.C. Hero and other later Greek inventors produced much larger and more lethal versions.

various kinds of huge catapults, dart throwers, and crossbows. Though such weapons were widely used in ancient times, most were abandoned and largely forgotten in Europe in the centuries following the collapse of the western Roman Empire in the fifth century A.D. and did not reappear until the eleventh century when medieval armies began to use them in siege warfare.

Laying Modern Science's Foundation Stones

Medieval times also saw the preservation by Arabic scholars of other aspects of ancient Greek science that Europe had lost during the social and cultural disruptions attending the fall of Rome. Eventually, these ideas were transmitted to the thinkers of the European Renaissance, who passed them along to the modern world. Underlying this ancient scientific legacy were two essential features of the scientific process—first, a fervent curiosity about the workings of nature, and second, the view that those workings are explainable in logical, material terms. Building on these tenets, modern scientists learned to confirm, modify, or reject existing theories, old and new, through rigorous examination and testing, in short, to apply the scientific method. In this way, asserts the noted science historian Marshall Claggett, "the foundation stones quarried, faced, and laid in Greek antiquity have provided the surest support for the scientific structure raised in modern times." [17]

CHAPTER 2

Democritus: The First Atomic World View

What is the world made of? This was one of the principal and profound questions that the early Greek scientists tried to answer, and Democritus was one of only two of them whose answer was essentially correct. The search for an underlying unity, the *physis*, had led Thales and others to propose that such substances as water and air comprise the fundamental basis for all physical, material things, or matter. Building on the ideas of his mentor, Leucippus, Democritus proposed instead that all matter is composed of tiny, indivisible seeds or particles called atoms; hence Leucippus and Democritus are credited with the invention of the atomic theory and referred to as the first "atomists." Very few of their colleagues or successors accepted the idea. The two men had stumbled on a concept that was too far ahead of its time to be accepted into the scientific mainstream. But their work was important because their notion of atoms was revived and developed by later ancient writers, who in turn passed it along to later ages.

Incredibly, Democritus's perfection of the atomic theory, though an achievement of immense proportions, was only one among the many accomplishments of his long, rich, and productive life. Possessed of a brilliant and fantastically versatile mind, he delved into an encyclopedic range of interests and researches, theorizing and writing in depth about mathematics, astronomy, biology, medicine, geography, philosophy, human psychology, and ethics. The third-century A.D. Greek biographer Diogenes Laertius listed among Democritus's works *The Great Cosmos, On the Planets, On Nature, On Reason, On the Senses, On the Soul, On the Criteria of Logic,* and *Ethical Reflections,* to name only a few.

Unfortunately, these and Democritus's other treatises are lost and all that remains are a few fragments, along with some brief synopses of his theories in the works of later writers. Modern science historians are unanimous in bemoaning this loss. "Democritus was indeed a universal mind who embraced the whole knowledge of his time," remarks Giorgio de Santillana, "and the loss of his works is a tragedy of history."[18] Benjamin Farrington goes further, saying that "the loss of his works is probably the most serious in the all but universal ruin that has overwhelmed the record of the earlier thinkers among the Greeks."[19] Thus, it may not be an exaggeration to say that had Democritus's major works survived, the evolution of scientific thought might have been very different.

"I Came to Athens and No One Knew Me"

Almost nothing is known about Democritus's childhood, except that he was born about 460 B.C. in Abdera, a small but prosperous town in Thrace, the then rustic Greek region bordering the northern Aegean Sea. It is perhaps ironic that one of the most brilliant minds produced in ancient times hailed from what was then

In this depiction of one of Democritus's legendary endeavors, he examines a dead animal in hopes of discovering the source of bile, then seen as one of the most essential bodily fluids.

seen as an intellectual backwash. In fact, people in Athens and other larger and more renowned Greek cities joked about Abderites being "backward" and "simple-minded."

This reputation was probably undeserved, for, although much of Thrace was indeed culturally backward at the time, Abdera's cultural and spiritual roots were in the highly civilized and cosmopolitan region of Ionia; the town had been founded a little less than a century before by emigrants from the Ionian city of Teos attempting to escape domination by the Persians, who had seized control of Asia Minor. In any case, Abdera produced not only Democritus, but also the noted philosophers Protagoras (fifth century B.C.) and Anaxarchus (fourth century B.C.). And it is unlikely that the local society that nurtured these men was markedly less enlightened than that of Athens.

Yet it was to Athens, then the acknowledged cultural center of the Greek world, that many young artists, philosophers, and scholars were drawn; for there they might meet and mingle with the greatest thinkers of the day and perhaps gain both knowledge and fame. Democritus, it appears, was no exception. Exactly when he paid his first visit to Athens is unknown, but it was probably as a young man shortly after his father's death. According to Diogenes, Democritus early had the urge to travel and

Nestled in a wooded area within sight of the famous Athenian Acropolis, this legendary garden was a favorite meeting place for philosophers and other thinkers.

being a third son and thus entitled to only a small share of the family inheritance, he chose to take it in money [instead of property] in order to pay his travel expenses. . . . Democritus's share was over one hundred talents [a great deal of money, since at the time one talent was equal to 6,000 silver coins called drachmas], which he spent in its entirety.[20]

On reaching Athens, Democritus sought out the famous sage Socrates, who was probably about ten years older than he, but for reasons unknown the younger man did not introduce himself. Perhaps he was shy or felt uncomfortable in a large city filled with strangers. The only surviving description of the visit by Democritus himself consists of the cryptic phrase, "I came to Athens and no one knew me."[21]

Over the next few years, Diogenes writes, Democritus traveled far and wide. First he journeyed to Egypt to learn about geometry from the local priests, who supposedly possessed a great deal of mathematical knowledge. Then he moved on to Persia, which then encompassed the much older lands of Sumeria and Babylonia, whose priest-scholars were also known for their accumulated knowledge. It is even possible that Democritus reached distant India, then rarely visited by inhabitants of the Mediterranean world. In his own words, "I am the most widely traveled man of all my contemporaries, and have pursued inquiries in the most distant places; I have visited more countries and climes [climates] than anyone else, and have listened to the teachings of more learned men."[22]

The "Full" and the "Empty"

Did Democritus learn the basic tenets of his most important theories from the foreign scholars he met during his travels? A few modern scholars have suggested that he picked up the idea of atoms from Indian sages.[23] However, though it is remotely possible that he heard versions of the theory elsewhere, there is no doubt whatsoever that his own version was largely an elaboration of the work of Leucippus, perhaps a native of Miletus, who was about the age of Democritus's father.

It appears that Leucippus's theory of matter was in large degree a reaction to some of the ideas of the Pythagoreans. They claimed that nature's underlying primary substance is changeless and indestructible. With that much Leucippus agreed. But the Pythagoreans also held that the underlying *physis*, whatever its true nature might be, is continuous or all-encompassing, that is, it occupies all of space without interruption. The Greeks called this continuous quality of matter a *plenum*. To Leucippus, the concept of a *plenum* did not satisfactorily explain how the *physis* could give rise to the great diversity of natural substances.

The starting point of Leucippus's and Democritus's atomic theory was the concept that the primary substance of matter, though changeless and indestructible, is not continuous. Instead, that substance is composed of two properties, roughly translated from the Greek as the "full" and the "empty." The full is matter, made up of an infinite number of particles, or atoms, that are too tiny to be seen; the empty is the void (a vacuum) that separates the atoms from one another. Furthermore, the theory stated, although atoms are alike in substance, they have different shapes, sizes, and arrangements. What people perceive as the multiplicity of objects and substances in nature are manifestations of varied and diverse groupings of atoms of various sizes and shapes. Objects come into existence when atoms come together; objects change their forms when atoms regroup; and objects pass out of existence when atoms disperse.

This bust, like others supposedly of Democritus, was made long after his death; his actual appearance is unknown.

One of Democritus's major contributions to this theory was an explanation of exactly *how* atoms "come together" to form the millions of diverse substances seen in nature. The sixth-century A.D. Greek philosopher Simplicius recorded this fascinating hypothesis:

The atoms are at war with one another as they move along in the void, owing to their dissimilarity and their other differences, and as they move they collide and are interlaced in a manner which makes them touch and be near to one another, but never really produces any single existence out of them: for it is quite absurd to suppose that two or more things could ever become one. The reason why the atoms for a certain time remain in combination he [Democritus] believes to be because they fit into and grasp one another: for some of them have uneven sides, and are hooked, some are concave, and some convex and others with innumerable varieties of shape. He thinks then that they retain hold of one another and remain in combination until some stronger necessity from what surrounds them comes and shakes them and scatters them apart. And he speaks of this coming into being and its opposite separation not merely with reference to animals, but also plants and worlds and generally about perceptible bodies.[24]

An Atomic Worldview

Democritus was not content merely to describe atoms and their random movements. He also boldly applied the atomic theory of matter to the earth and the heavens, creating a cosmology quite different from that later developed by Plato, Aristotle, Ptolemy, and others in the scientific mainstream. According to Democritus, the creation was a random process. As the atoms moved chaotically through the void, often colliding with one another, the larger ones tended to "grasp one another" and thereby to cluster together. This continued until the heavier, "earthy" substances formed the center of things (the earth itself). Meanwhile, the lighter atoms continued to swirl, by now in a circular motion, around the earth and gave rise to lighter substances such as air and fire; but a few random heavier lumps remained up above and these became the planets and other heavenly bodies.

Not only are the heavenly bodies and other solid objects composed of atoms reacting within the "empty," said Democritus, but so are all other aspects of nature, even those normally thought of as intangible. Regarding such sensations as temperature, color, texture, smell, and taste, for instance, he states in a surviving fragment, "By convention there is sweet, by convention there is bitter, by convention hot and cold, by convention color; but in reality there are only atoms and the void." [25] In a surviving fragment from his own largely lost work, *On the Senses,* the father of botany, Theophrastus, describes some of Democritus's views on sensations:

> He argues that none [of the sensory qualities] has objective reality, but that all of them are effects of our sensuous faculty as it undergoes alteration. . . . Nor does he regard hot and cold as having an objective nature; they are merely a matter of configuration [certain groupings of atoms]. . . . Anything sour, he holds, is composed of atoms that are angular, tiny, thin, and twisted. By its sharpness it slips in and penetrates everywhere. . . . But sweet consists of atomic figures that are rounded and not too hard; it softens the body by its gentle action.[26]

31

Even the soul, Democritus suggested, was made up of atoms, specifically of a very light, subtle, and mobile variety. In wispy congregations, these special atoms float through the air until they enter people's and animals' bodies. Thereafter, respiration, or breathing in and out, keeps them from escaping. Aristotle explained it this way:

> In animals that breathe, according to Democritus, their respiration has the result of preventing the soul from being

Democritus, pictured in this modern engraving, proposed that death results when the atoms comprising the soul escape the body.

squeezed out from the body. . . . For in the air there are many such [spherical and extremely tiny] particles which he identifies with mind and soul. When we breathe and air enters, these enter along with it, and by withstanding the pressure they prevent the soul in the animal from being forced out. Democritus thus explains why life and death are bound up with respiration. Death occurs when the surrounding air [in the lungs] presses upon the soul to such a degree that the animal can no longer respire. . . . Death is the departure of [the atoms comprising the soul] because of pressures from the air that surrounds them.[27]

Of course, Democritus's version of how atoms combine was off the mark and his earth-centered cosmology and supposition that sensations arise from differing atomic shapes was equally flawed. Moreover, modern science has so far found no evidence to support his conception of the soul (nor anyone else's for that matter). Yet it is striking that he was right in the essential concept of atoms and the fact that they do combine in diverse ways to form nature's substances. From this fact, he correctly reasoned that matter cannot be created from nothing or destroyed into nothing, a principle accepted by modern physicists. Moreover, his description of a primeval cloud of matter out of which the heavier substances condensed to form the heavenly bodies, including the earth, and his idea that the heavenly bodies undergo life cycles is remarkably similar to modern views of the birth and death of solar systems. As Farrington puts it, considering the state of knowledge in Democritus's day, his worldview "remains one of the supreme achievements of scientific thought."[28]

The Truest Cause of All

In explaining so many diverse natural phenomena and encompassing so many fields of scholarly study and endeavor, Democritus's version of the atomic theory was hugely and masterfully comprehensive. It is unlikely, therefore, that he conceived, wrote about, and introduced it in the span of a year, five years, or even ten years. Indeed, he almost certainly continued to expand and perfect it throughout his whole adult life, which, fortunately for him, was long and fulfilling.

After ending his travels, perhaps when he was in his forties, Democritus settled down permanently in his home town of Abdera. According to various ancient sources, he had spent all of his inheritance abroad, so at first he lived in poverty and had to accept handouts from one of his brothers. But Democritus's fame as a scientist and writer grew rapidly and he learned to turn his new-found prestige into wealth. Assuming that Diogenes' account is accurate,

> there was a law [in Abdera] . . . to the effect that no one who had squandered what he had inherited from his father was to be buried within the city precincts. Knowing of the law and fearing to be at the mercy of envious and un-scrupulous executors [those who would dispose of his re-mains and estate after his death], Democritus gave a public reading of *The Great Cosmos,* the best of all his books. As a result they [the citizens] raised a stipend of five hundred talents for him, and they gave him some valuable bronzes [statues and figurines] in addition.[29]

From that time on, presumably, the adamant atomist enjoyed the financial freedom and public respect that allowed him to write and conduct research in comfort.

It is possible that Democritus was still hard at work when death overtook him at about the age of one hundred. (Living this long was a highly unusual occurrence, since average life expectancy was then not much over thirty.) According to some ancient sources, he re-alized the end was coming but managed, with the aid of hot com-presses, to hold on for the three days it took his sister to return from a religious festival. Then he stopped the treatment and allowed nature to take its course.

Another later bust of Demo-critus. After years of traveling abroad, he returned to and settled permanently in his native town of Abdera.

It is tantalizing to wonder how the staunchly materialistic Demo-critus faced the prospect of death. Did he, like most Greeks of his time, believe that the soul survives in an afterlife? Or did he adhere to a strictly material conception in which, at the moment of death, the atoms making up the soul escape the body's restraints and float back into nature's random and indestructible mix of particles and voids? A fragment of his writings contains a statement that appears to support the second view: "Some men, with no understanding of how our mortal nature dissolves [at death], but keenly aware of the ills of this life, afflict life still more with anxieties and fears by making up false tales about the time that comes after the end." [30] However, a brief excerpt from Diogenes' treatise appears to combine both views in a simple, unique, and appealing way: "The end of human action he [Democritus] declares to be tranquillity; which . . . consists in an enduring calm and strength of the soul, free from fear, superstition, or other emotion. He also calls it well-being." [31]

This modern painting of Democritus attempts to capture his legendary cheerful demeanor.

Whatever Democritus thought about death, he apparently thoroughly enjoyed life; ancient sources claim that he advocated being cheerful even in the face of misfortune, and that he practiced what he preached, earning him the nickname of the "laughing philosopher." Happy or not, his life was certainly uncommonly productive. And measured against his own famous quip—"I would rather discover one true cause [of nature's workings] than gain the kingdom of Persia"—it was also an unqualified success. [32] For his description of atoms, with all of its wrong guesses and imperfections, had laid bare for future investigators the truest and most fundamental cause of all.

CHAPTER 3

Plato: The Creation of the Universe

The name of Plato, the first important post-Socratic thinker, looms large in the philosophical, scientific, and literary heritage of Western civilization. His studies ranged over many and varied subjects, most prominently politics, laws, and ethics, about which he wrote a large number of treatises that posterity has deemed among the most brilliant and important ever written. He was also fascinated by various aspects of science. His major scientific work, the *Timaeus,* a comprehensive description of the formation of the universe, the shapes and compositions of the heavenly bodies, and the forces governing universal motions, exerted a profound influence on scholarly thinking in ancient, medieval, and early modern times.

Plato was not a true scientist in the modern sense. For one thing, he conducted no systematic experiments to test his theories about the earth and heavenly bodies; moreover, his cosmic model was a hodgepodge of mechanical, religious, moral, and mystical elements that now more rightly belong to the fields of philosophy and theology or to the false science of astrology than to the sciences of astronomy and cosmology. Yet one must keep in mind that in Plato's time science and philosophy had not yet separated into distinct disciplines. In attempting to construct their philosophical worldviews, he and most of his colleagues thought it perfectly natural to combine what are now seen as unrelated or incompatible scientific and nonscientific ideas. Also, Plato's work was part of a major shift in emphasis within Greek philosophy that began during the final years of the lifetime of his mentor, Socrates (the end of the fifth century B.C.); this shift was away from the mainly mechanical conceptions of the *physis* and the cosmos proposed by pre-Socratic thinkers like Thales, Anaxagoras, and Democritus, toward more political and ethical concerns. In general, then, Plato's importance to the history of science lies not with the specifics of his theories, which turned out to be mostly wrong, but with the great impact of these ideas on future generations of scientists.

Plato was born in 427 B.C. into a distinguished Athenian family. Because his father, Ariston, and mother, Perictione, were well-to-do aristocrats, and also because Athens was the cultural hub of the Greek world, the best and most learned tutors available must have instructed the boy. In fact, Athens's unique cultural and political position in Greek affairs did more than afford young Plato an excellent education. As it happened, he grew up in a turbulent and fateful transitional period in which the city's fortunes, prestige, and whole way of life were taking a rapid turn for the worse; and this situation became one of the two major influences that shaped his political and ethical ideas and ideals.

As a child, Plato could not help feeling awe for and great pride in Athens's power and cultural splendor. A mere half century before his birth, the city, the world's first democracy, had, along with another powerful city-state, Sparta, led the other tiny Greek states in a stunning victory over the Persians, halting their attempted invasion of Europe. In succeeding decades, Athenian statesmen, the most dynamic among them Themistocles, Cimon, and Pericles, managed to consolidate over one hundred Greek states into a prosperous empire controlled by Athens; and Pericles used much of the wealth that flowed into the city's coffers to champion the work of sculptors and other artists and to erect magnificent buildings, including those on the city's central hill, the Acropolis. For a brief historical moment, Athens was the most beautiful, enlightened, and powerful city in the Mediterranean world.

A reconstruction of the magnificent temples and other buildings erected on the Athenian Acropolis in the late fifth century B.C.

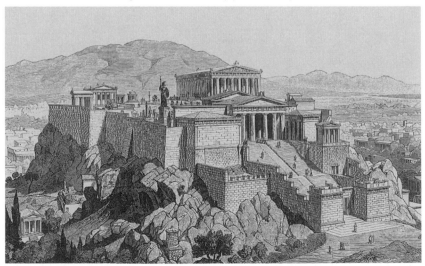

But during Plato's boyhood, Athens's golden age was already rapidly waning. In 431 B.C., the city and its allies went to war with Sparta and its own allies; this so-called Peloponnesian War turned out to be a devastating twenty-seven-year-long conflict that engulfed and exhausted all the Greek states.[33] After suffering horrendous casualties and economic ruin, Athens lost the war and for a time its cherished democracy, too. All of this largely senseless bloodshed and societal upheaval left the young Plato, who hated violence and injustice, disillusioned and bitter. His anger and moral revulsion that Greek leaders of his time seemed more interested in *de*structive than *con*structive endeavors is apparent in this excerpt from his dialogue, the *Gorgias:*

> The people say that they have made the city great, not seeing that the swollen and ulcerated condition of the state is to be attributed to these elder statesmen; for they have filled the city full of harbors and docks and walls and revenues and all that, and have left no room for justice and temperance. And when the crisis of the disorder comes, the people will . . . applaud Themistocles, Cimon, and Pericles, who are the real authors of their calamities.[34]

Disheartened by Injustice

Plato later reacted to the deplorable condition into which Athens and the rest of Greece had fallen by writing the *Republic,* the most famous, widely read, and influential of all his works. In it, he depicted what he saw as an ideal society, a hypothetical commonwealth in which an elite group of individuals would rule wisely and justly. According to scholar Robert Downs:

> Plato conceived the Greek city-state as the highest known form of society, but one obviously suffering from serious internal weaknesses. Consequently, the problem to which Plato addressed himself was: What changes should be made in the organization of the city-state to eliminate strife and factionalism, provide the greatest good for all its inhabitants, and achieve a stable order? . . . In effect, the governing elite in Plato's *Republic* lives under a communistic regime. Its members are required to share their goods, houses, and meals. . . . [His] ideal commonwealth would thus be ruled by a gifted class of men and women who have sacrificed property and material comforts, who procreate in the best interests of the state, who subordinate passion and individuality to the spirit and to reason.[35]

The other major influence on Plato's early life and formulation of his worldview was his relationship with the philosopher Socrates. They must have met when Plato was a child, for his uncle, Charmides, and his mother's cousin, Critias, were by then already Socrates' close friends and followers. Around 407 B.C., when Plato was twenty, he too became an ardent disciple of the odd little man who wandered the streets barefoot, engaging people in conversation and argumentation and admonishing them always to seek justice and truth. Socrates' unique method of seeking these values, asking people a series of questions and weighing each answer with logic, reason, and uncompromising honesty, left an indelible imprint on Plato's intellect and personality. Socrates "captured Plato's imagination," writes Nickolas Pappas, of the City College of New York,

> as a symbol of the questioning philosopher, who follows an investigation wherever it may lead. For Plato, Socrates' courage, honesty, and integrity always overlap with his intellectual virtues, especially his devotion to the truth for its own sake, together with an uncanny cheerfulness in the face of everyone's failure at reaching that truth. This deep unity of philosophy and morality may have been Socrates' most persistent influence on Plato.[36]

In 399 B.C., the Athenian state prosecuted, tried, and executed Socrates on the trumped-up charge of corrupting the morals of young people.[37] Plato was disgusted and disheartened by this act against one he termed "by far the best, the wisest, and most just" person he had ever known. The depiction in the *Republic* of a state devoid of injustice and of the misuse of political power was as much a reaction against the pointless death of his friend as it was against war and political and moral corruption. In his often-quoted *Seventh Letter,* Plato wrote about his feelings of disillusionment and confusion, saying that

> some of those in power brought my friend Socrates . . . to trial before a court of law, laying a most iniquitous [grossly unjust] charge against him. . . . As I observed these incidents and the men engaged in public affairs, the laws too and the customs, the more closely I examined them . . . the more difficult it seemed to me to handle public affairs. . . . The result was that, though at first I had been full of a strong impulse towards political life, as I looked at the course of affairs and saw them being swept in all directions

39

This celebrated painting by the eighteenth-century French artist, Jacques Louis David, dramatically captures the last moments in the life of Plato's friend and mentor, Socrates.

by contending currents, my head now began to swim; and . . . I postponed [a public career] till a suitable opportunity should arise.[38]

It turned out that no such suitable opportunity to enter formal politics ever did arise for Plato. Shortly after Socrates' death, he went to live in another city-state, Megara; and in the years that followed he traveled extensively, visiting Egypt and Greek cities in Italy and Sicily. Sometime in the 380s B.C., he returned to Athens, bought a plot of land, and on it established the Academy. The first true university in the modern sense, the school was designed primarily as a training ground for a new breed of statesmen, in Plato's view men of deep personal conviction, commitment to virtue and good works, and a strong sense of justice. It was his hope that the institution might provide the first generation of enlightened rulers who would usher in a new and better world. This naive dream never became reality, of course; yet the Academy endured, remaining an important center of philosophical and other scholarly studies for some nine hundred years.

The Incorruptible and Ageless Forms

During his long tenure as head of the Academy, Plato perfected his worldview and produced the bulk of his works, most of which, including the *Timaeus*, were in the form of dialogues among two or more characters. At the core of all of his thinking and writing, both scientific and otherwise, rested his version of nature's *physis*— his theory of forms. Underlying the physical world perceived by the senses, he held, is an invisible realm of pure forms and ideas. According to this view, the cosmos was put together by a divine craftsman, the Demiurge, who began with perfect ideas and plans for constructing all the various objects and elements of the earth and heavens. The visible, touchable versions of these things are only imperfect replicas of the original and ideal forms. Plato

Plato converses with a student at the Academy, the school of higher learning the philosopher established in Athens sometime in the 380s B.C.

offered the analogy of a carpenter who visualizes in his mind's eye the table he plans to build; the carpenter reproduces this mental idea as closely as possible when actually making the table, but because of limitations inherent in the tools, materials, and his own skills, the finished product does not and cannot measure up exactly with the ideal form still distinctly clear in his mind. Moreover, Plato postulated, the invisible world of ideas and forms is real and eternal, while the visible world is only an impermanent and imperfect shadow cast by that underlying reality. George Sarton clarified it this way:

The sensible world is submitted to corruption and death, but the ideas, being immaterial, are incorruptible and ageless. The world of ideas is real and permanent. The idea is not only the essential reality of a thing, it is also its definition and name; hence, we are given at one and the same time the tools of knowledge and its valid elements. The ideas are not fancies, but beings, living and eternal; they are forms, patterns, wombs, standards.[39]

Plato, pictured here, proposed the "theory of forms," which held that the visible world is only a kind of illusion.

The main aim of science, then, according to Plato, is to investigate and understand these perfect, eternal ideas. And the successful philosopher-scientist is one who can see beyond the insubstantial and deceiving appearances of the visible world and into the realm of these forms.

Plato's Cosmology

Plato's theory of forms provided the structural underpinning for the cosmology he proposed in his *Timaeus*. To begin with, because the whole idea of perfect original forms presupposed a divine craftsman, his cosmic model also incorporated the Demiurge. Was the universe "always in existence and without beginning," he asks, or "had it a beginning?"[40] His answer is that the universe had a clear-cut beginning, although he envisioned that beginning differently than modern scientists do. Cosmologists now feel that all the universe came into being suddenly in a titanic explosion, the so-called "big bang"; whereas Plato held that someone or something had to have created the original forms of the creatures and objects populating the universe, as well as their visible replicas. "All sensible things," he writes, "are in a process of creation and created" by a divine intelligence.[41]

It is important to stress that Plato did not envision the Demiurge as an omnipotent being who created matter out of nothingness, as the Judeo-Christian god supposedly did. Plato's creator is "a benevolent craftsman," science historian David Lindberg explains, who, like the carpenter in the analogy,

> struggles against the limitations inherent in the materials with which he must work in order to produce a cosmos as good, beautiful, and intellectually satisfying as possible. The Demiurge takes a primitive chaos, filled with the unformed material out of which the cosmos will be constructed, and imposes order according to a rational plan. This is not creation from nothing . . . for the raw materials are already present and contain properties over which the Demiurge has no control; nor is the Demiurge omnipotent, for he is constrained and limited by the materials that he confronts.[42]

Plato cautioned that human beings are equally constrained and limited by their inability to see or communicate with the Demiurge; it is fruitless, therefore, to try to define his exact nature, for "the father and maker of all this universe is past finding out; and even if we found him, to tell of him to all men would be impossible."[43]

Plato then goes on to describe the structure of the universe, saying that its motions are circular because a circle, a two-dimensional slice of a sphere, is a perfect geometric form.[44] Indeed, he says, the universe itself is a gigantic sphere and the heavenly bodies, including the earth, are smaller spheres. The earth rests, unmoving, at the center and the sun, moon, planets, and other celestial bodies revolve around it. To this mechanical structure, Plato adds several spiritual and mystical elements (some borrowed from or influenced by Babylonian and Egyptian astrology), among them the idea that the cosmos possesses a soul that pervades all matter; that the stars and planets, being the most sublime replicas of the Demiurge's original forms, are godlike entities whose unerring movements in their orbits guarantee the regularity of nature; and that humans' souls derive from stars and return to them after death.

The Respect of Later Generations

The *Timaeus* was the most popular and widely read of Plato's works in ancient times. Moreover, after the disintegration of Greco-Roman civilization in the fifth and sixth centuries A.D., it was both the only Platonic text and the only major Greek philosophic-scientific work known to early medieval Europe. By then, Plato had acquired an exalted (and obviously highly distorted) reputation as a nearly infallible ancient seer; so the cosmic model postulated in the treatise came to be revered and accepted as gospel truth by medieval scholars, who saw its Demiurge and cosmos-wide soul as manifestations of the Christian creator-god.

Critical views by modern scholars on the later impact of the *Timaeus* have been divided. Literary scholars have tended to praise the work's style and to see it as a masterful and compelling example of mythology and/or imaginative fiction. Science historians, on the other hand, have been more critical, pointing out that the blind acceptance of its mystical and largely inaccurate doctrines long impeded the progress of true science. The most renowned science historian of all, George Sarton, was also the most outspoken in condemning the legacy of the *Timaeus,* calling it "a monument of unwisdom and recklessness." Much of the "astrologic nonsense" that still survives in Western culture, said Sarton, originated with the Babylonians and other pre-Greek peoples and was then perpetuated in and legitimized by Plato's cosmology. "The influence

Later European scholars revered Plato as a fountainhead of wisdom and avidly studied his treatise, the Timaeus.

of the *Timaeus* upon later times was enormous and essentially evil. . . . I cannot mention any other work whose influence was more mischievous. . . . Errors and superstitions are never more dangerous than when they are offered to us under the cloak of science." [45]

Whatever its influence on later ages, for Plato himself the *Timaeus* was simply part of his systematic attempt to show that humans live within an ordered, reasonable, and moral universe and that they should try to be just as reasonable and ethical in their own affairs. He wanted to show how the ideal human social and moral order he had advocated in the *Republic* reflected the organization and morality already manifest in divine intelligence. The *Timaeus,* written near the end of his life, while he continued to oversee the Academy, was intended to be the first third of a trilogy recounting the entire history of the universe and humanity up to his time. But he never finished the second and third parts of the larger work, abruptly switching his attention to the *Laws,* a massive compendium of proposed laws for governing a just and moral state.

The *Laws* turned out to be Plato's last work, for shortly after finishing it he died, in about 347 B.C., at the age of eighty. The exact circumstances of his passing are uncertain; but according to popular tradition, he attended a wedding feast and fell asleep in his chair, and when his hosts tried to wake him the next morning, they found that he had died peacefully during the night. All of his works survived him to the present, a record unmatched by any other ancient author and a testimonial to the high level of respect and reverence succeeding generations accorded him and his ideas.

CHAPTER 4

Aristotle: The Classification of Animals

No person of the ancient world had a greater impact on the subsequent development of philosophy, science, and knowledge in general than Aristotle. Out of genuine feelings of awe and respect, dozens of generations of Western thinkers referred to him simply

Aristotle, the most influential philosopher-scientist of ancient times.

as "the philosopher"; the Italian Renaissance scholar Dante, himself one of the greatest intellectuals Europe ever produced, called him "master of those who know"; and Charles Darwin, the eminent and hugely influential nineteenth-century naturalist, remarked that the modern founders of his own field were mere schoolboys compared to "old Aristotle." These and countless other tributes to Aristotle over the centuries can be attributed to the extremely wide range of his interests and researches and the fact that he made detailed, logical, and sometimes profound written observations in every major branch of learning. Indeed, scholar Robert Downs comments,

> Aristotle was unquestionably the greatest collector and systematizer of knowledge produced by the ancient world. Prior to the Renaissance in modern Europe, he was the first to undertake a systematic survey of all existing knowledge in all fields of science. His works are an encyclopedia of the learning of the ancient world, and except in physics and astronomy, he made important contributions in practically every subject touched.[46]

Aristotle's influence on the future growth of knowledge was both negative and positive. On the one hand, many of his doctrines, such as the earth-centered universe, were incorrect and, as happened with Plato's *Timaeus,* their almost blind acceptance by later European scholars long impeded progress in astronomy and cosmology. Moreover, as scholar Renford Bambrough points out,

> the sheer weight of his [Aristotle's] authority often inhibited his successors from making their own independent contributions to thought. In logic and the natural sciences especially, his disciples were slow to see when the time had come to go further than their master, or in a different direction.[47]

On the other hand, some of Aristotle's ideas and works, particularly in the field of biology, brilliantly anticipated modern discoveries. And although his scientific treatises are now quaint antiques no longer used as texts by science students, his philosophical ideas and works remain alive and relevant after more than two millennia. "Not only is he essential reading in any study of the history of western philosophy," writes Aristotelian scholar G. E. R. Lloyd, "but on many problems, in both moral philosophy and metaphysics, what he has to say also has continuing importance to practical philosophers."[48]

"The Mind"

The man whose thinking would so strongly influence later Western intellectual development himself felt the influence of the rich scientific and philosophical tradition already established in Greece by the time of his birth. His father, Nicomachus, was a practitioner of that tradition, earning a notable reputation as physician to King Amyntas II of Macedonia, then a politically and culturally backward kingdom in extreme northwestern Greece. In the years following his son's birth, in 384 B.C. at Stagira, a town on the Chalcidic peninsula (on the northern rim of the Aegean Sea), Nicomachus encouraged the boy to pursue intellectual endeavors. From his father, Aristotle learned a great deal about the natural sciences, including biology, and perhaps also about the theory and practice of medicine.

In 367 B.C., his parents having recently died, the seventeen-year-old Aristotle journeyed to Athens and enrolled at Plato's Academy, where the young man lived and studied for the next twenty years. In ancient times, a number of stories circulated claiming that Plato and Aristotle developed a personal dislike for each other and frequently

Aristotle converses with his teacher and friend, Plato, in the center of this famous painting, "The School of Athens," by the fifteenth-century Italian master Raphael.

fought during these years. However, no factual evidence supports this contention. Modern scholars feel these false tales developed much later, after both men were dead, and were based on the fact that Aristotle often disagreed with some of his mentor's ideas.

The younger man rejected Plato's theory of forms, for instance. Aristotle agreed that the "forms" of various objects and creatures exist; but he held that these were defining principles, or blueprints, inherent within the objects and creatures themselves, not intangibles floating in a separate realm, as Plato had postulated. In the words of scholar Louise Loomis:

> Plato had two worlds in conflict, the terrestrial [earthly] world of visible but unreal, transitory [impermanent] objects, and the celestial world of invisible but real and immortal spiritual existences. Making two worlds out of one, Aristotle insists, merely multiplies the things to be explained. Our present, visible world is the only one, and is itself real and eternal, an indissoluble combination of matter and form. . . . No need to imagine visitors from a spiritual realm coming down to create the [elements of the visible world], which have always existed. [According to Aristotle] there is nothing indeed to show that a spiritual realm exists.[49]

In fact, despite Aristotle's differences with Plato about the nature of the forms and other concepts, all available evidence suggests that the two men sincerely respected each other and got along exceedingly well. For example, Plato affectionately referred to Aristotle as "the mind" and "the reader"; the younger man's earliest written works were dialogues imitating the structure and expressing the ideas of the older man's own famous dialogues; and in some of his later works, Aristotle spoke highly of his former teacher.

Crisscrossing the Aegean

When Plato died in 347 B.C., his nephew, Speusippus, took over as director of the Academy. Perhaps because he did not care for Speusippus's approach to studying philosophy, Aristotle, now about thirty-seven, left the school.[50] Crossing the Aegean, Aristotle made his home for a time in the small town of Assos (near Atarneus), on the northwestern coast of Asia Minor. There, aided by Theophrastus, from the neighboring island of Lesbos, whom he had known at the Academy, he helped to run a small branch of that university dedicated to spreading Greek philosophy in the region. But soon afterward the takeover of local politics by a pro-Persian faction hostile to Greek influences forced Aristotle and the others to move to Theophrastus's home on Lesbos.

During this period, Aristotle married a local woman, Pythias, for whom he apparently had strong feelings of love and respect. (This is evidenced by the fact that, although when she died young he married another woman, Herpyllis, who bore him a son and daughter, many years later he ordered in his will that Pythias's remains be placed beside him in his tomb.) Also during this period, Aristotle wrote important sections of his *Politics,* part of which, like Plato's *Republic,* sketches the framework of an ideal state. Of all the world's peoples, Aristotle states in the work, only the Greeks have that special combination of intelligence, courage, and spirit possessed by "natural rulers"; and if only the Greek states could achieve unity, they could easily rule the world.

The tenets of this arrogant, Greek-centered doctrine strongly appealed to Aristotle's most famous student, Alexander, crown prince of Macedonia, who would later be called "the Great." In recent years, Macedonia had undergone a remarkable growth in military power and political influence under its intelligent and dynamic king, Philip II, Alexander's father. In 343 B.C., Philip asked Aristotle to come to the Macedonian capital, Pella, and tutor the prince, then thirteen. The philosopher agreed to do so and spent the next several years in Macedonia.

In 336 B.C., Philip was assassinated and Alexander ascended the throne of Macedonia, which by this time controlled most of Greece.[51] No longer needed in Pella, Aristotle returned to Athens and there, in 335 B.C., established his own school, the Lyceum, a public institution dedicated to the god Apollo. It soon became known as the "peripatetic" school in reference to the *peripatos*, or covered walkway, under which the philosopher and his students strolled each morning while he lectured them.

Regularly utilizing the Lyceum's steadily growing library and zoo, both invaluable aids to research, in the following twelve years Aristotle produced the bulk of his important writings. Of these, almost all that were published and that ancient scholars such as the Roman orator Cicero praised as highly eloquent, stylish, witty, and thoroughly readable, are lost. The large corpus of Aristotle's surviving works consists mainly of his notes, rough drafts of his lectures, and notations made of his lectures by his students. Un-

Aristotle tutors the young Alexander of Macedonia, who will eventually succeed his father, King Philip II. Aristotle taught Alexander that it was natural for Greeks to rule non-Greeks, who were inferiors.

fortunately, these treatises are for the most part very scholarly, dry, and formal. As noted Aristotelian scholar A. E. Taylor puts it, "his language bristles with technicalities, makes little appeal to the emotions, disdains graces of style, and frequently defies the simplest rules of composition." [52]

His Cosmic Clockwork

Though often difficult and tedious to read, Aristotle's surviving works nevertheless have served the vital function of transmitting his main ideas to later ages. Of his principal scientific ideas, among the most important, considering their impact on later generations of scientific thinkers, are those dealing with cosmology. His cosmic model, while similar in many ways to that of Plato and the Pythagoreans, was much more sophisticated and complex. For instance, Aristotle agreed with his predecessors that all matter was composed of the basic elements of earth, water, air, and fire; but he maintained that these were imperfect and changeable and therefore only existed on earth and its immediate vicinity. By contrast, the heavens, being eternal and incorruptible, were composed of a special fifth element—the "quintessence" or "ether."

Also like his predecessors, Aristotle advocated that the earth rests at the center of the universe and is a sphere. But in addition to accepting the earth's sphericity on faith, because "a sphere is the most perfect form," he offered tangible evidence to support the claim, citing the unambiguous curve of the earth's shadow on the moon during lunar eclipses:

> As it is, the shapes which the moon itself each month shows are of every kind—straight, gibbous, and concave—but in eclipses the outline is always curved: and, since it is the interposition of the earth [between sun and moon] that makes the eclipse, the form of this line will be caused by the form of the earth's surface, which is therefore spherical. [53]

Aristotle's model for the overall structure of the universe was also more sophisticated than the ideas of earlier scholars. The Pythagoreans had proposed that the heavenly bodies moved as if they were attached to three huge concentric and invisible spheres. Eudoxus, one of Plato's colleagues at the Academy, expanded this relatively simple model into a complicated one featuring twenty-seven spheres. Each celestial body, Eudoxus claimed, was connected to more than one sphere, each such sphere accounting for a single, specific motion of that body. He postulated one sphere

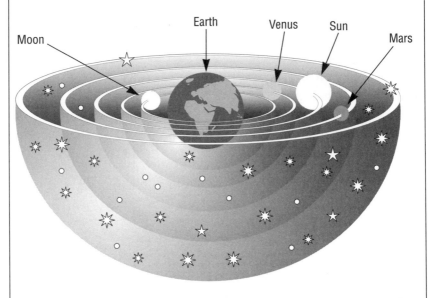

Eudoxus's and Aristotle's Heavenly Spheres

Moon   Earth   Venus   Sun   Mars

This simplified cutaway view of the celestial system proposed by Eudoxus and expanded by Aristotle shows the central Earth encased by concentric spheres, each carrying a heavenly body; the outermost sphere holds the stars.

for the fixed stars, three each for the sun and moon, and four each for the five planets then known. A few years later, Eudoxus's pupil, Callipus, produced a still more complex model having thirty-four heavenly spheres.

Even thirty-four spheres did not satisfy Aristotle, however, who raised the number to at least fifty-five. In his view:

> It is necessary, if all the spheres combined are to explain the observed facts, that for each of the planets there should be other spheres . . . which counteract those already mentioned and bring back to the same position the outermost sphere of the star which in each case is situated below the star in question; for only thus can all the forces at work produce the observed motion of the planets.[54]

Aristotle further proposed that the heavenly spheres were made of ether, which was crystalline and transparent, explaining why they were invisible to human eyes. His unseen spheres were physically connected in a complex mechanical construction, making up a universe with interlocking parts, each part moving according to natural laws. Aristotle's basic vision of the cosmos as an earth-centered "cosmic clockwork" made of ether, though wrong in most of its main points, seemed so logical to so many people that it dominated the discipline of astronomy for nearly two thousand years.

The "Father of Biology"

From a purely scientific standpoint, Aristotle's work in biology was far superior to his efforts in astronomy. Although some of the biological conclusions he drew were off the mark, a great many more were correct or at the very least visionary. He collected literally thousands of observations and specimens, fueling his pioneering studies in nearly all the main branches of biologic inquiry, including comparative anatomy, ethology (animal habits), embryology (pre-birth development), geographic distribution of animals, and ecology (relation of animals to their environment). For these reasons, modern science historians generally recognize him as the "father of biology."

Aristotle would not have been able to wade through and form opinions about the vast amount of data he collected in these areas without an efficient method of organization and inquiry. So he conceived a general procedure of

This Roman depiction of Aristotle incorrectly depicts him without a full beard, the style followed by all men in his time.

scientific research that followed some basic steps. This was in some ways an ancient precursor of the modern scientific method. According to Aristotelian scholar Theodore James:

> In general, Aristotle follows this procedure:
> 1. He determines accurately the subject-matter of the investigation, and its problematic [problem to be solved].
> 2. He describes historically the diverse solutions proposed to the problem under consideration.
> 3. He inserts reasons for doubting the previous solutions.
> 4. He indicates his own solution with appropriate evidence and reasoning.
> 5. He refutes the other solutions proposed.[55]

Unfortunately, while Aristotle stressed the importance of evidence, he failed to appreciate that experimentation is almost always the best method of finding it. Often, his evidence consisted merely of personal deductions made from simple observations; and sometimes he did not even go to the trouble of observing, but made baseless assumptions and called them evidence.

Yet on those occasions when he made careful observations, and especially when he conducted crude experiments, Aristotle made astute and largely correct deductions. His most fruitful biological experiments involved the dissection of at least fifty different animal species.[56] Among his original and correct discoveries were that whales and dolphins are mammals, like people and dogs; that some fish have bones and others cartilage; that cows have four-chambered stomachs; that birds and reptiles are anatomically similar; and that embryonic chicks have beating hearts. About the gestation of a baby chick in its egg, he wrote:

> With the common hen after three days and three nights there is the first indication of the embryo. . . . Meanwhile the yoke comes into being, rising towards the sharp end, where the primal element of the egg is situated, and where the egg gets hatched; and the heart appears, like a speck of blood, in the white of the egg. This point beats and moves as though endowed with life, and from it two vein-ducts with blood in them trend [move] in a convoluted course. . . . A little afterwards the body is differentiated, at first very small and white. The head is clearly distinguished, and in it the eyes, swollen out to a great extent. . . . When the egg is now ten days old the chick and all its parts are distinctly visible.[57]

Unfortunately, because of religious taboos Aristotle could not dissect human bodies, which caused him to make certain erroneous assumptions about human anatomy and physiology. His mistakes included the notions that the heart is the seat of intelligence; that the main job of the brain is to cool the heart; that veins and arteries are essentially the same; and that some living things "spontaneously generate," or grow directly from substances such as mud and rotting garbage.[58]

Creatures With and Without Blood

Aristotle's most important contribution to the field of biology was his introduction of a system of zoological classification, or grouping of animal species by type. His version remained the most influential until Swedish scholar Carolus Linnaeus published his pioneering work in the field in 1758. Aristotle began by rejecting earlier systems that classified species in categories such as land versus water animals, or winged versus wingless creatures; for though a whale lives in water, he pointed out, it is related to land mammals rather than fishes; and there are both winged and wingless ants.

Instead, Aristotle divided the animal kingdom into two parts: those creatures with blood and those without, roughly corresponding to vertebrates (animals with backbones) and invertebrates.

Aristotle, pictured here deep in thought, has often been called the "father of biology." He dissected at least fifty different animal species and also observed that embryonic chicks have beating hearts.

Each of these further broke down into genera (roughly corresponding to modern phyla), and each genus contained several related species. In classifying these genera, Aristotle correctly recognized that the various animal groups follow a gradual progression from the least to the most complex and advanced, with human beings occupying the highest position on the zoological ladder:

> Nature proceeds little by little from things lifeless to animal life in such a way that it is impossible to determine the exact line of demarcation [between forms], nor on which side thereof an intermediate form should lie. . . . And so throughout the entire animal scale there is a graduated differentiation in amount of vitality and in capacity for motion.[59]

His five invertebrate genera included (in ascending order): zoophytes (corals, sponges), insects, mollusks, crustacea (lobsters, shrimps), and cephalopods (octopi, squids); and his six vertebrate genera: fishes, reptiles and amphibians, birds, sea mammals, land animals, and humans. He also made some brilliant deductions in such areas as animal migrations, predators and prey, the extinction of some species because of adverse environmental factors, and modes of sexual reproduction and embryonic development. These insights and achievements of Aristotle's illustrate, in George Sarton's words, "the magnitude of his biologic genius. He was not only the first great one in his field . . . but he remained the greatest for two thousand years."[60]

An Enemy of the State?

During Aristotle's years at the Lyceum, as he calmly worked on his *History of Animals, On the Parts of Animals,* and other biological studies, the forces of his downfall were already gathering in a distant land. In the same year the Lyceum had begun operation, Aristotle's former pupil Alexander had led a Greek invasion force eastward into Asia; and over the course of the following decade the young conqueror had dismantled the massive Persian Empire and brought all the lands stretching from the Mediterranean coast to distant India under his sway. During these years, most of Greece remained under Macedonian control, causing deep resentment in Athens and other formerly independent city-states. Not surprisingly then, when Alexander suddenly died in faraway Babylon in 323 B.C., a wave of anti-Macedonian feeling and rebellion swept through Greece.

Aristotle and some of his followers reluctantly leave Athens after the philosopher's trial. His countrymen questioned his loyalty, citing his earlier close association with Macedonia's King Alexander.

Because Aristotle had been Alexander's friend and tutor, the Athenians now looked on the philosopher as an enemy of the state; they brought him to trial, forcing him to flee northward to the island of Euboea, where he owned an estate. There, a few months later, in November 322 B.C., shaken and bitter, he died at the age of sixty-two. His old friend and colleague Theophrastus succeeded him as director of the Lyceum. Meanwhile, Aristotle's son, Nicomachus, began compiling and editing his father's lectures, an act that ended up having far reaching consequences. Had these works not been preserved, future ages would have known Aristotle, one of the most important figures in the history of science, by little more than his name and reputation.

CHAPTER 5

Theophrastus: The Foundations of Botany

If Aristotle was the father of biology, Theophrastus amply deserves the title of father of botany, the study of the plant kingdom. He was not the first Greek botanist, for others before him, including the famous fifth-century historian Herodotus, had described various plant species and otherwise dabbled in the field. Yet they were mere amateurs compared to Theophrastus. He was the first to study and write about plants in a thorough and systematic way and also the first to classify the known species of plants, as Aristotle had done with animals.

Theophrastus's major contributions were two large botanical works—*On the History of Plants* and *On the Causes of Plants,* the most important writings in the field from his day to the end of the Middle Ages. In fact, after his death not a single significant discovery beyond his own occurred in the field of botany for over eighteen hundred years. "It is very strange," George Sarton remarks, "that so much botanical knowledge should have been accumulated by the end of the fourth century B.C., and that so little, if anything, was added to it in ancient times." [61] The reasons for this are unclear; but it is likely that most later ancient scientists saw Theophrastus as a nearly infallible sage whose works could not be improved on.

Ironically, despite his exalted reputation, Theophrastus did not influence early European scholars directly, primarily because his works were not translated into Latin until the fifteenth century. However, *in*directly his influence was extensive. An anonymous first-century B.C. treatise, *On Plants,* and the *Materials of Medicine,* a work on the medicinal uses of plants by the first-century A.D. Greek physician Dioscorides, were both widely read and revered in medieval times; and both texts relied heavily on Theophrastus's writings and observations. Thus, it is not inappropriate to view Theophrastus's works on plants, in combination with Aristotle's on animals, as the climax of the study of natural history before the modern era.

Inheritor of the Lyceum

Theophrastus, whose original name was Tyrtamus, was born about 370 B.C. at Eresos on the Aegean island of Lesbos. Like so many other aspiring Greek philosophers, scientists, and artists of that era, as a young man he traveled to Athens to acquire knowledge and the companionship of the brightest minds of the time.

He found both by enrolling at Plato's Academy. There Tyrtamus met Aristotle, some fourteen years his senior, whose later classification of animals may have inspired the younger man's own classification of plants (Plato may also have provided this inspiration). After Aristotle and Tyrtamus became close friends, the former began calling the latter by the nickname of Theophrastus, meaning "divine of speech," a reference to his clear and eloquent speaking manner; and the name stuck.

Theophrastus, the "father of botany," pictured here, attended Plato's Academy and later succeeded Aristotle as head of the prestigious Lyceum in Athens.

When Plato died, Theophrastus joined Aristotle in moving to Assos, on the coast of Asia Minor, where for a time they studied and taught in a smaller version of the Academy. After Aristotle moved to Macedonia in 343 B.C. to tutor the young crown prince Alexander, Theophrastus may have followed. Eventually, both scholars ended up back in Athens, where Theophrastus became a prominent member of his friend's new school, the Lyceum. The two became so close that when Aristotle died in 322 B.C. he left Theophrastus the guardianship of his children; bequeathed him his library, garden, and personal writings; and named him as his successor as director of the Lyceum.

It was during his subsequent thirty-five-year-long occupancy of that post that Theophrastus produced most of his writings. These were not only about plants, for, like Democritus and Aristotle, he was interested in and pursued a wide range of subjects. And also as in the case of Aristotle, most of Theophrastus's polished and popular writings have been lost, the majority of the surviving ones taking the form of notes *for* his lectures or notes taken *of* his lectures by his students.

An Expansive Sense of Humor and a Dislike for Superstition

The important exception is the *Characters,* a compilation of thirty insightful and delightfully humorous sketches of common character types of his day. Composed about 319 B.C., the work became extremely influential later. In medieval times students of rhetoric used it as a study piece; and beginning in the 1600s it became the blueprint for similar works by English, French, and other European humorists. The following excerpt, from the section titled "Bad Timing," demonstrates the author's acute powers of observation and sharp and expansive sense of humor.

Although Theophrastus passed on a number of superstitions common in his day, he did not take most folk beliefs seriously, preferring ideas backed by evidence.

The man with bad timing is the sort who . . . sings love songs to his girlfriend when she has a fever . . . shows up [in court] to give testimony after the case has already been decided. If he's a guest at a wedding, he launches into a tirade against women. When a man has just returned from a long journey, he invites him to go for a walk. . . . After people have listened and understand, he stands up to explain all over again. . . . When a slave is being beaten, he stands watching and tells the story of how a slave of his once hanged himself after being beaten in just this way. . . . When he wants to dance, he grabs a partner who is still sober.[62]

More relevant to Theophrastus's scientific mind-set was his character sketch titled "Superstition." This piece reflects his dislike for the then widespread acceptance of various superstitions, most of which he recognized had no basis in fact and only stood in the way of scientific endeavor; it also constitutes a priceless record of some of the most common folk beliefs of his day.

The superstitious man is the sort who, when he meets a funeral procession, washes his hands, sprinkles himself with water from a shrine, puts a sprig of laurel in his mouth [all religious purification rituals] and walks around that way all day. If a weasel [associated then with bad luck, as a black cat is today] crosses his path he goes no further until someone passes between them, or he throws three stones over the road. . . . If owls hoot as he passes by, he becomes agitated and says "mighty Athena!" [the goddess whose symbol and mascot was the owl] before he goes on. . . . If he ever notices someone at the crossroads wreathed in garlic [it was commonly believed that crossroads were favorite haunts of evil spirits and that garlic protected against such spirits], he goes away, takes a shower, summons priestesses and orders a deluxe purification. . . . If he sees a madman or epileptic, he shudders and spits down at his chest [the ancient Greek equivalent of knocking on wood].[63]

Identifying the Types and Parts of Plants

However much Theophrastus disliked them, some superstitions inevitably found their way into his scientific treatises about plants. Among these were the beliefs: that some plants had to be collected by day, others by night; that if a person broke religious taboos after collecting herbs, these plants lost their effectiveness; that gardeners should face east while lifting out roots; and that garlic should be eaten before collecting certain plants. To his credit, he was skeptical of most of these wrong-headed ideas and included them only because he found them quaint and fascinating. On the other hand, like his friend Aristotle, he readily incorporated the concept of spontaneous generation, which later scientists would prove false, because it was universally accepted in his day.

Yet these occasional inaccuracies seem trivial in comparison to the staggering amount of accurate, insightful, and useful information about the plant kingdom that Theophrastus recorded for posterity. His detailed identification of the types and parts of plants alone was enough to establish him as a first-rate scientific observer and investigator. He described nearly 550 species in all, most of them from Europe, Asia Minor, and Palestine. However, a fair number were indigenous to Persia, India, and other more distant lands; he learned about these from reports sent to him by those several of his students who joined Alexander the Great's eastern expedition expressly for that purpose. Among the plants these field researchers collected and described to their mentor were the cotton plant, banyan tree, cinnamon, pepper, myrrh, frankincense, and the Persian apple. Theophrastus's description of the last of these demonstrates the plentiful amount of information he often supplied about a single species; concise, detailed, factual, and systematic in the modern scientific sense, it reads like a modern-day encyclopedia article:

> This tree has . . . thorns like those of the pear or whitethorn, which however are smooth and very sharp and strong. The "apple" is not eaten, but it is very fragrant, as also is the leaf of the tree. And if the "apple" is placed among clothes, it keeps them from being moth-eaten. It is also useful when one has drunk deadly poison; for being given in wine it upsets the stomach and brings up the poison. . . . The seed is taken from the fruit and sown in spring in carefully tilled beds, and is then watered every

Theophrastus lectures some of his students on the properties of plants. He left behind detailed descriptions of hundreds of species, some from as far away as India.

62

fourth or fifth day. And, when it is growing vigorously, it is transplanted, also in spring, to a soft well-watered place, where the soil is not too fine. . . . Of the flowers . . . those which have, as it were, a distaff [pistil] in the middle are fertile, while those that have it not are infertile.[64]

Propagation and Pollination

Impressive as this and Theophrastus's other descriptions of various plant species are, they represent only a small portion of his output on botany. His encyclopedic knowledge of the subject ranged from the effects of climate and cultivation, to plant diseases, to the processes and techniques of plant propagation, or reproduction, including germination, budding, and grafting and growing cuttings. To this last and crucial category, plant propagation, he devoted the whole of Book II of his *History of Plants,* which begins with the following systematic and astute observations:

> The ways in which trees and plants in general originate are these; spontaneous growth, growth from seed, from a root, from a piece torn off, from a branch or twig, from the trunk itself, or . . . from small pieces into which the wood is cut up. . . . All plants start in one or other of these ways, and most of them in more than one. Thus the olive is grown in all the ways mentioned, except from a twig; for an olive-twig will not grow if it is set in the ground, as a fig or pomegranate will grow from their young shoots. . . . The fig grows in all the ways mentioned, except from root-stock and cleft wood; apple and pear grow also from branches, but rarely. . . . There are quite a few plants which grow and are brought into being more easily from the upper parts, as the vine is grown from branches; for this, though it cannot be grown from the "head," yet can be grown from the branch, as can all similar trees and undershrubs, for instance . . . rue, gilliflower [carnation], bergamot-mint, tufted thyme, [and] calamint. So the commonest ways of growth with all plants are from a piece torn off or from seed; for all plants that have seeds grow also from seed.[65]

This excerpt, representing only a minute portion of Theophrastus's remarks on plant propagation, establishes not only his keen powers of observation, but also that he engaged in a fair amount of practical experimentation. Careful observation likely led him to one of his greatest discoveries—the process of pollination. And through gardening experiments (conducted both by himself and his students) he learned techniques of hand-pollination (artificial fertilization). "With dates," he explained,

> it is helpful to bring the male to the female; for it is the male which causes the fruit to persist and ripen. . . . The process is thus performed: when the male [date] palm is in flower, they at once cut off the spathe [leaves forming the base] on which the flower is . . . and shake the bloom with the flower and the dust over the fruit of the female, and, if this is done to it, it retains the fruit and does not shed it. In the case of both the fig and the date it appears that the "male" renders aid to the "female." [66]

In time, this valuable piece of knowledge was largely lost to European gardeners and had to wait over two thousand years to be rediscovered.[67]

An Enormous Output

Besides his character sketches and many writings on plants, Theophrastus also produced a treatise on minerals, rocks, and gems, the study of which is today referred to as petrography. Part of the treatise has survived and, per usual, his descriptions are systematic, detailed, and largely free of superstition and unscientific information and jargon; moreover, he often provides information derived from direct experiments (again, either his own or those performed by others). In describing the chemical reactions that occur when lead reacts with vinegar (part of the then common process of producing "white lead," a pigment used in painting), for instance, he wrote:

> A piece of lead the size of a brick is placed over vinegar in an earthenware vessel. When the lead has acquired a [rust-like] layer, which usually happens in ten days, they open the vessel and scrape off the decayed part. The process is then repeated again and again until the lead is entirely consumed. They take what has been scraped off and keep pulverizing it in a mortar and filtering it. What finally settles to the bottom is white lead.[68]

These and Theophrastus's thousands of other observations of and theories about the natural world required many years of painstaking research and writing. Besides this enormous output, he was almost constantly preparing and delivering lectures and running the Lyceum, which at times may have had an enrollment as high as two thousand. Enthusiastic and relentless in his efforts, he may well have been what people refer to today as a "workaholic," for one of the sayings tradition attributes to him is "Nothing costs us so dear as the waste of time."

A nineteenth-century French engraving of Theophrastus shows a parchment scroll listing the titles of some of his best-known works.

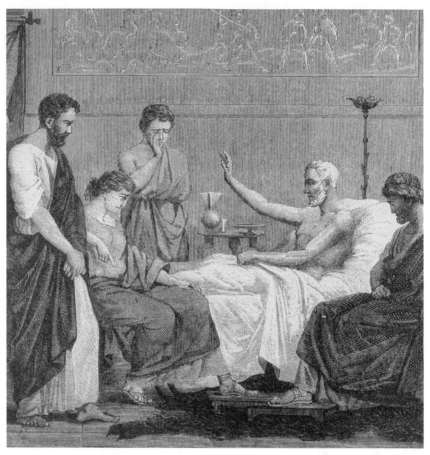

On his deathbed, Theophrastus delivers his famous last words, "We die just when we are beginning to live." Almost two thousand years passed before botanists began to surpass him.

An Exceptional Life

Considering that he viewed time as a precious commodity, Theophrastus was fortunate in enjoying an exceptionally long life. Still active and productive when he died about 285 B.C. at the age of eighty-five, he no doubt would have liked at least one more long lifetime to devote to learning and teaching. "We die just when we are beginning to live," he supposedly said on his deathbed. His will, which has survived, attests that he was also generous and concerned with perpetuating the Lyceum and its systematic pursuit of knowledge:

> The garden and the walk and the houses adjoining the garden, all and sundry, I give and bequeath to such of our

enrolled friends as may wish to study literature and philosophy there in common, since it is not possible for men to be always in residence, on condition that no one alienates the property or devotes it to his private use, but so that they hold it like a temple in joint possession, as is right and proper, on terms of familiarity and friendship.[69]

Following his final wish, his grateful heirs buried him, appropriately, in the Lyceum's garden among the plants that had so long and so thoroughly fascinated him.

CHAPTER 6

Archimedes: The Application of Mechanical Principles

Science historians agree that Archimedes, who lived and worked in the early years of the Hellenistic period of Greek science, was the outstanding mathematician of ancient times; and it would be no exaggeration to call him one of the greatest inventors and engineers of *all* times. Among his most important contributions to science, and certainly his most famous, were his elegant mathematical proofs of key mechanical principles and the marvelous machines he constructed utilizing those principles. "Some say," wrote Pappus of Alexandria in the fourth century A.D., "that Archimedes of Syracuse mastered the principles and theory of all [the branches of mechanics]. For he is the only man down to our time who brought a versatile genius and understanding to them all." [70] Indeed, if Archimedes could somehow be instantly transported to the present, it is conceivable that he could, after a brief refresher course in modern math and physics, fully understand and perhaps even elaborate on the ideas of scientific giants like Albert Einstein.

These lavish assessments of Archimedes' genius are firmly supported by the evidence, part of which consists of the stories told about him by other ancient writers. The most famous such accounts are those of the first-century A.D. Greek historian Plutarch, who, in his biography of the Roman general Marcellus, described some of Archimedes' fabulous machines and other feats. Even if some of these astounding stories are exaggerated, the contents of Archimedes' own scientific writings are not. The majority of these works have fortunately survived and constitute the primary evidence of his genius. His *On the Sphere and Cylinder, Measurement of a Circle, On the Equilibrium of Planes, The Sand-Reckoner, On Floating Bodies,* and other works consist of clear, logical, and largely correct demonstrations of some of the most important mathematical and mechanical concepts, including the fundamental laws of levers and floating bodies. In each of these works, he presents his propositions and proofs in a straightforward, step-by-step manner that is virtually no different from that employed in modern math and science textbooks. Considering that he had no sophisticated measuring and calculating tools to work with, the brilliance of his methods and the accuracy of his conclusions are truly amazing.

A Disdain for Practical Application

Archimedes was born about 287 B.C. at Syracuse, then a splendid and powerful independent Greek city-state on the island of Sicily. According to a remark in his *Sand-Reckoner,* his father, Pheidias, was an astronomer who attempted to measure the sizes and distances of the sun and moon. Plutarch claims that Archimedes was related to Hiero II, king of Syracuse from about 265 to 216 B.C.; and it appears that the scientist was also well-acquainted with Hiero's son and successor, Gelo. Thus, it is fairly certain that Archimedes hailed from a well-to-do and prestigious family that provided him with an excellent early education.

Archimedes' advanced schooling took place at the famous Museum in Alexandria, Egypt, where he may have studied under the pupils of the renowned ancient master of geometry, Euclid. There too, the young scholar met and became friends with the mathematician Conon of Samos, Conon's pupil, Dositheus of Pelusium, and the geographer-astronomer Eratosthenes (who later calculated

Archimedes, pictured here with a compass and a diagram of Syracuse, viewed practical engineering applications as beneath his dignity. He much preferred abstract math.

the earth's circumference with an error of less than 1 percent); Archimedes later sent his treatises to these men, presumably to get their opinions, and/or addressed them directly in the introductions to these works.[71]

According to some ancient sources, while in Egypt Archimedes invented the water screw, often called "Archimedes' Screw," a sort of pump designed to make it easier to raise water, a backbreaking endeavor when done by muscle power alone. It consisted of a pipe twisted in the form of a corkscrew and confined within a cylinder; as the pipe rotated around its axis, the screw twists drew water from one level (such as a lake or stream) and carried it up to a higher level (such as a reservoir or irrigation ditch). Other ancient sources suggest that Archimedes invented the water screw after returning to Syracuse, where he faced the challenge of draining bilge water from the hold of a huge ship belonging to his friend, King Hiero. Wherever Archimedes invented the device, thereafter people in various parts of the world used it for irrigation and other purposes; and in fact, some of the inhabitants of today's poorest countries still employ a version of it.

It is unknown when Archimedes departed Egypt and returned to Syracuse, but once back in his native city he apparently rarely, if ever, left it again. He would have preferred to lock himself away in an ivory tower, so to speak, and there spend his life reflecting on abstract mathematical principles; for ironically, despite his invention of the water screw, he initially had no strong

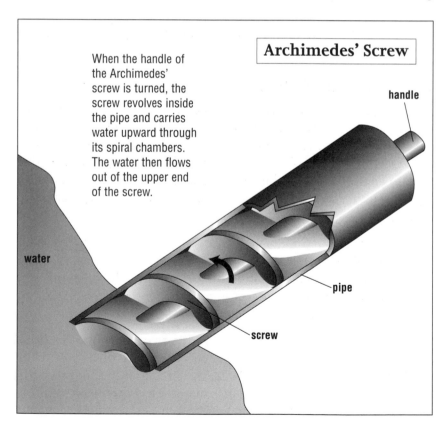

Archimedes' Screw

When the handle of the Archimedes' screw is turned, the screw revolves inside the pipe and carries water upward through its spiral chambers. The water then flows out of the upper end of the screw.

handle

water

pipe

screw

interest in mechanical contrivances. About Archimedes' love of theoretical science and disdain for its practical applications, Plutarch wrote:

> He was a man who possessed such exalted ideals, such profound spiritual vision, and such a wealth of scientific knowledge that, although his inventions had earned a reputation for almost superhuman intellectual power, he would not deign to leave behind him any writings on his mechanical discoveries. He regarded the business of engineering . . . as ignoble and sordid activity, and he concentrated his ambition exclusively upon those speculations whose beauty and subtlety were untainted by the claims of necessity. These studies, he believed, are incomparably superior to any others, since here the grandeur and beauty of the subject matter vie for our admiration with the cogency and precision of the methods of proof. Certainly in the whole science of geometry it is impossible to find more difficult or intricate problems handled in simpler and purer terms than in his works. . . . So it is not at all difficult to credit some of the stories which have been told about him; of how, for example, he often . . . would forget to eat his food or take care of his person.[72]

The Principles of Floating Bodies

But though Archimedes dreamed of dedicating himself to the pursuit of "pure" science, his patron, Hiero, saw such efforts as misdirected and a waste of valuable practical potential. Hiero fully recognized Archimedes' extraordinary mechanical aptitude and desired to exploit it for the benefit of their city and its people. Thus, says Plutarch, the king "often pressed and finally persuaded" the scientist

> to divert his studies from the pursuit of abstract principles to the solution of practical problems, and to make his theories more intelligible to the majority of mankind by applying them through the medium of the senses to the needs of everyday life.[73]

One of the most famous stories about the two men concerns how Archimedes discovered the fundamental concept of hydrostatics (the branch of mechanics that deals with pressures in fluids). Hiero had ordered a new crown of pure gold made. When it arrived he suspected that the contractor had cheated him by mixing some

Archimedes contemplates Hiero's crown and several weighted balls (on the floor), as the scientist prepares to perform his classic experiment demonstrating the property of density.

cheaper silver with the gold; and he asked Archimedes to confirm his suspicion without melting down the crown. While pondering the problem, Archimedes went to the public baths. Noticing how his and other people's bodies displaced the water in the pool, the solution suddenly came to him and he jumped up and ran home, still naked and shouting "Heureka!" ("I've found it!").[74]

Archimedes then conducted a classic experiment, based on his knowledge that a pound of silver takes up almost twice as much space as a pound of gold. According to a later ancient source, he took

> two masses of the same weight as the crown, one of gold and the other of silver. When he had done this, he filled a large vessel to the brim with water, into which he dropped the mass of silver. The amount of this when let down into the water corresponded to the overflow of water. . . . In this way he discovered what weight of silver corresponded to a given measure of water. . . . He then dropped a mass of gold in like manner into the full vessel and removed it. . . . This corresponded to the lessened quantity of the same

weight of gold compared with the same weight of silver. He then let down the crown itself into the vase . . . and found that more water flowed into the space left by the crown than into the space left by a mass of gold of the same weight. And so from the fact that there was more water in the case of the crown than in the mass of gold, he calculated and detected the mixture of the silver with the gold, and the fraud of the contractor.[75]

This experiment established that the force that buoys up a body suspended in a fluid equals the weight of the fluid the body displaces, the basis of what became known as the "Archimedes Principle"— that every substance has a certain density.[76] One of the inventor's subsequent practical applications of his discoveries about floating bodies was his design of ships that were unusually stable in the water and therefore less likely to turn over and capsize.

"I Can Move the World"

Archimedes also experimented with levers, a practical extension of the brilliant mathematical deductions he presented in his *On the Equilibrium of Planes*. The work's first three propositions state: "Weights which balance at equal distances are equal; unequal weights at equal distances will not balance but will incline towards the greater weight; and unequal weights will balance at unequal distances, the greater weight being at the lesser distance."[77] For example, two children of equal weight who sit at equal distances from the fulcrum (center point) of a seesaw will balance each other; if one child is replaced by a heavier one, the seesaw will tip downward under the heavier one; but if the heavier one moves closer to the fulcrum, the two children of unequal weights will balance. Archimedes provided elegant mathematical proofs for these commonly observed phenomena, as well as for other principles concerning the centers of gravity of various geometric shapes.

According to tradition, these calculations and conclusions about levers and equilibrium led Archimedes to brag to Hiero, "Give me place to stand on and I can move the world." What he meant, if indeed he ever said it, was that if he had a large enough lever, could place the earth on one end, and could stand on some imaginary other world to push on the other end, he could lift the earth using only the power of his own muscles. Supposedly, Hiero was intrigued and demanded a demonstration of a tiny force moving a great weight. According to Plutarch's famous account:

The machine composed of a "complex system of pulleys," which Archimedes had designed to impress King Hiero, is seen here pulling a ship toward shore.

Archimedes chose for his demonstration a three-masted merchantman [cargo ship] of the royal fleet, which had been hauled ashore with immense labor by a large gang of men, and he proceeded to have the ship loaded with her usual freight and embarked a large number of passengers. He then seated himself at some distance away and without using any noticeable force, but merely exerting traction with his hand through a complex system of pulleys, he drew the vessel towards him with as smooth and even a motion as if she were gliding through the water.[78]

Archimedes designed other fabulous machines, including the first known mechanical planetarium, with globes representing the moon, sun, and planets going through their complex motions. After his death, the Romans brought this device to their capital, where the great senator and orator Cicero saw it and described it in his *Republic*. It was "a remarkable contrivance," declared Cicero, because Archimedes

had devised a means whereby a single turning would preserve the unequal and varying speeds of the different motions. . . . [When someone rotated the sphere] the moon followed the sun on the bronze globe by a number of revolutions equal to the number of days by which it followed it in the sky itself. Thus there occurred an eclipse of the sun on the sphere, just as in the sky, and the moon passed into the region of the earth's shadow.[79]

Like a Mythological Giant

Perhaps the most famous, and certainly the most spectacular, of all Archimedes' mechanisms were the weapons used in Syracuse's defense against the Romans in 213–212 B.C. Hiero, long Rome's friend, had recently died and his successors allied themselves with Carthage, the empire opposing Rome in the current Second Punic War. When the Romans attacked Syracuse both by land and sea, Plutarch stated,

> Archimedes brought his engines to bear and launched a tremendous barrage against the Roman army. This consisted of a variety of missiles, including a great volley of stones [thrown by catapults larger and more lethal than any yet invented] which descended upon their target with an incredible noise and velocity. There was no protection against this artillery, and the soldiers were knocked down in swathes and their ranks thrown into confusion. At the same time huge beams were run out from the walls so as to project over the Roman ships: some of them were then sunk by great weights dropped from above, while others were seized at the bows by iron claws or by beaks like those of cranes, hauled into the air by means of counterweights until they stood upright upon their sterns, and then allowed to plunge . . . [until they were] dashed against the steep cliffs and rocks which jutted out under the walls, with great loss of life to the crews.[80]

So effective were the defenses Archimedes had designed that they struck fear into the hearts of the Roman troops. Constantly assaulted by huge devices wielded by an opponent they could not see, said Plutarch, they began to believe that they were fighting some kind of supernatural, rather than mortal, enemy. Eventually, they were "reduced to such a state of alarm that if they saw so much as a length of rope or a piece of timber appear over the top of the wall, it was enough to make them cry out, 'Look, Archimedes is aiming one of his machines at us!' and they would turn their backs and run."[81] Indeed, the Roman commander, Marcellus, was several times forced to order a retreat. He greatly respected his scholarly adversary, whom he reportedly paid the compliment of comparison with Briareus, a mythological giant with a hundr hands:

> We may as well give up fighting this geometrical Briareus, who uses our ships like cups to ladle water out of the sea, who has whipped our *sambuca* [a large siege engine] and driven it off in disgrace, and who can outdo the hundred-handed giants of mythology in hurling so many different missiles at us at once.[82]

Archimedes positions a mirror so that its reflected light will burn the sails of Roman ships, one of the legendary feats attributed to him.

Archimedes sits in deep concentration during the final moments of the Roman siege of Syracuse. Within seconds, the soldier entering the room, unaware of the old man's identity, will kill him.

Like Hiero, Marcellus wanted to take personal advantage of Archimedes' genius, for with this mechanical wizard on its side, Marcellus reasoned, Rome might win its war against Carthage quickly and decisively. Just prior to the final assault on the city, therefore, the Roman commander gave strict orders that Archimedes should not be harmed. During the attack, a Roman soldier found the scientist sitting quietly, lost in thought, or as Plutarch puts it,

> engrossed in working out some calculation by means of a diagram, and his eyes and his thoughts were so intent upon the problem that he was completely unaware that the Romans had broken through the defenses, or that the city had been captured.[83]

Tragically, the soldier failed to recognize Archimedes and slew him.

The Power of Mathematical Analysis

Afterwards, Marcellus openly expressed his deep regret for the loss of Archimedes. The general made sure that the scientist received a proper burial and also befriended his surviving relatives;

moreover, hearing that Archimedes had earlier expressed the desire that his tomb bear a certain inscription, Marcellus saw to it. The simple inscription showed Archimedes' favorite geometrical theorem, one he personally viewed as his greatest discovery—the ratio of the volume of a cylinder to that of a sphere.

About a century and a half later, when Cicero was serving as a financial official in Sicily, then a Roman province, he searched diligently in Syracuse for Archimedes' tomb. He finally found it, overgrown with briers and forgotten, near one of the city's gates. Piously, Cicero restored the tomb; but over time it was forgotten again and never rediscovered. Luckily, Archimedes' mathematical and mechanical principles did not meet a similar fate; they survived, and as science historian David Lindberg eloquently puts it, they reveal

> the thoroughness and the extraordinary skill with which he geometrized nature [i.e., explained nature's workings in geometrical terms]. Many scientific problems continued to resist solution by mathematical methods [in the centuries that followed], but Archimedes remained a symbol of the power of mathematical analysis and a source of inspiration for those who believed that mathematics was capable of ever greater triumphs.[84]

CHAPTER 7

Ptolemy: The Mapping of the Earth and Heavens

Ptolemy (pronounced TAH-luh-mee) was the greatest geographer of ancient times. His book, *Guide to Geography,* was a work of immense importance from a historical point of view because it significantly contributed to shaping the world view of early Europe. His maps, copied and recopied by scholars in different eras and lands, remained standard for some fourteen centuries and were the principal guiding force behind the development of the modern science of cartography, or mapmaking. The early pioneers of Europe's age of exploration fully accepted the authenticity of Ptolemy's maps, not realizing that they contained a number of major errors; Christopher Columbus, for example, based his belief that he could reach Asia by sailing westward on the fact that Ptolemy extended Asia much too far eastward on the map. And as late as 1775, most scholars still clung to Ptolemy's mistaken belief that the Indian Ocean was bounded by a southern continent.

No less influential than Ptolemy's geographical work on the thinking of later generations was his great astronomical work, which he and his contemporaries referred to as the *Syntaxis,* or *Mathematical Compilation.* Later, in the ninth century, when Arab scholars translated it from the Greek, they correctly recognized it as the greatest work of astronomy produced in antiquity; so they called it *al-majisti,* meaning "The Greatest." Eventually, when the work was translated into Latin, the Arabic title mutated to *Almagesti,* and finally to *Almagest,* by which it is commonly known today.

The *Almagest* is a long, complex, and elegantly crafted synthesis of the prevailing geocentric astronomical views of Ptolemy's day, which had crystallized during the more than four centuries that separated him from the time of Plato and Aristotle. Ptolemy's work was, in a very real sense, the culmination of the development of ancient Greek astronomy. He gave the earth-centered cosmic model a workable and seemingly highly authoritative mathematical

CLAVDII PTOLEMAEI

PHELVDIENSIS ALEXANDRINI
ALMAGESTVM SEV MAGNAE CONSTRVCTIONIS
MATHEMATICAE OPVS PLANE DIVINVM
LATINA DONATVM LINGVA
AB GEORGIO TRAPEZVNTIO VSQVEQVAQ.
DOCTISSIMO.
PER LVCAM GAVRICVM NEAPOLIT. DIVINAE
MATHESEOS PROFESSOREM EGREGIVM
IN ALMA VRBE VENETA ORBIS REGINA
RECOGNITVM
ANNO SALVTIS M D XXVIII LABENTE

Nequifpiam alius Calcographus/Venetiis aut ufquá locorum
Venetæ ditionis impune Almageftum hunc imprimat per De/
cennium/Senatus Veneti Decreto cautum eft.

This is the cover page of a 1528 publication of Ptolemy's great astro-
nomical work, the Almagest. *Although many of his ideas and calculations*
were incorrect, he showed that the heavens could be described in
mathematical terms.

underpinning that guaranteed its universal acceptance until the
sixteenth-century Polish astronomer Nicolaus Copernicus proved
it wrong. More than any other book, remarks astronomer and
science historian Owen Gingerich, the *Almagest* demonstrated
to early Europeans "that natural phenomena, complex in appearance, could be described by relatively simple underlying reg-
ularities in a mathematical fashion that allowed for specific
quantitative predictions." [85]

An Egyptian, a Greek, and a Roman

Although Ptolemy achieved lasting fame as a geographer and astronomer, almost nothing of a definite nature is known about his personal life. What little *is* known has been pieced together from passing remarks made in his own works and in those of later writers, most of them Arab scholars who revered him as an unerring fountainhead of ancient wisdom. According to these sources, he was born about A.D. 100 at Ptolemais Hermii, a town located approximately eighty miles northwest of the Egyptian city of Thebes.[86] His full name was Claudius Ptolemaeus (his last name being a Latinized version of the Greek name Ptolemy), indicating that he was a Roman citizen; this was not unusual, since at the time Egypt was a Roman province. Thus, Ptolemy was an Egyptian by birth, a Greek by heritage, and a Roman by political status.

Despite the form of his name, there is no evidence to suggest that Ptolemy was a member of the Ptolemaic dynasty, the famous family that had ruled Egypt in the last few centuries B.C.[87] On the one hand, the name Ptolemy was extremely common in the many Greek communities that then existed in Egypt. On the other, the name might also have been used to signify that he came from the "Ptolemaic" district of his home city, or perhaps that he long resided in the Ptolemaic district of Egypt's capital, Alexandria.

Historians generally presume that Ptolemy lived in Alexandria because it is almost certain that he worked at that city's famous university, the Museum. However, one ancient source suggests that he lived in Canopus, a small town about fifteen miles east of Alexandria. It is possible that both suppositions are correct; perhaps he spent much of his time in the capital and occasionally escaped to the seclusion of a country house in Canopus. All Ptolemy himself said of his whereabouts was that he made his observations "in the parallel of Alexandria," meaning in that city's approximate latitude north of the equator.

The Great Map Atlas

In fact, determining the latitude of various cities and other geographical sites was among Ptolemy's major considerations in compiling his *Guide to Geography*. He probably produced this work between A.D. 150 and 160, although there is no way to be certain. The basic idea of latitude (horizontal map lines) and longitude (vertical map lines) was not new. It had been described by earlier Greek Alexandrian scholars, most prominent among them Eratosthenes (ca. 296–194 B.C.) and the great astronomer Hipparchus (ca. 190–120 B.C.), who suggested using such lines to plot points on maps. Ptolemy's *Guide* was the first known and greatest ancient example of a map atlas that represented length and breadth in a complex system of degrees of latitude and longitude. The treatise is divided into eight books (or sections), the first of which discusses the principles of applying mathematics to geography and mapmaking and also includes a thumbnail sketch of the length and breadth of the inhabited world; the next six books list the lat-

The Greek astronomer Hipparchus, inventor of longitude and latitude, makes observations for the great star catalogue he is credited with compiling.

itude and longitude of some eight thousand geographical locations; and the last book gives estimates for the longest day of the year in various latitudes and longitudes.

From a modern vantage, the *Guide* is a hodgepodge of right and wrong statements and assumptions supported by geographical measurements ranging from the nearly accurate to, more often than not, the highly *in*accurate. For instance, Ptolemy correctly states that Africa (which he calls Libya) is joined to Asia by the Sinai Peninsula (between modern Egypt and Israel), and that Africa, Asia, and Europe are all connected. "Libya is separated from Europe," he says in Book VII,

The Greek scholar Eratosthenes, who correctly calculated the earth's circumference.

> by the strait [of Gibraltar, which the ancients called the Pillars of Hercules], and while directly joined to Europe [at that point], is yet indirectly connected with it through Asia. For Asia is continuous with both Europe and Libya, being contiguous with them in the east [i.e., the Near East].[88]

By contrast, Ptolemy places the equator too far north. And he incorrectly asserts that the Indian Ocean is landlocked: "The whole Indian Sea, along with the gulfs that are connected with it . . . is entirely surrounded by land."[89] Many of his individual measurements are just as erroneous because he began with a figure for the earth's circumference that was about 30 percent too small. Eratosthenes had earlier arrived at the nearly correct figure of 25,000 miles, but Ptolemy made the mistake of adopting the figure calculated by another Greek predecessor, Poseidonius (ca. 130–50 B.C.), namely 18,000 miles. This fundamental error naturally threw most of Ptolemy's calculations off, a mistake that ended up profoundly affecting world history. By underestimating the size of the Atlantic Ocean (and overestimating the size of Asia) he helped inspire Columbus and other explorers to attempt transatlantic crossings, then highly risky ventures.

But it would be overcritical and unfair to labor on Ptolemy's mistakes. Considering the crude tools and unreliable sources he had to work with, his geographical efforts were quite extraordinary. As scholar Robert Downs points out:

This fifteenth-century map, based on one from Ptolemy's Guide to Geography, *incorrectly shows India as an island floating in the "Indicum Mare," or Indian Sea. This was only one of Ptolemy's geographical errors.*

In his time exact data were extremely scarce. He studied itineraries [travel schedules and accounts] of Roman officials and merchants. He estimated distances by the average of time required for journeys or voyages between certain points. He compared authorities. But in the end, such vague sources could produce only rough approximations, and the farther removed the localities were from known places, the more unreliable the figures became.[90]

Thus, Ptolemy's geographical theories were essentially sound; and it is entirely feasible that, if he had possessed accurate data and precise measuring instruments, he might have produced results as reliable as those of modern geographers.

Ptolemaic Astronomy

Most of Ptolemy's astronomical theories were not nearly as sound as his geographical ones, however. Admittedly, the complex mathematical system he worked out in his *Almagest* was capable of making fairly precise forecasts of future planetary positions, which helped to convince succeeding generations of scholars that his cosmic model was the correct one. Indeed, his system was so elegant and logical and seemed to explain so much so well that it was accepted almost as holy writ for the next fourteen centuries. Yet this system was almost entirely imaginary. The reality was that Ptolemy had begun with an *in*correct model, an earth-centered one, and then, in a brilliant demonstration of mathematical prowess, managed to devise a scheme explaining the movements of the heavenly bodies within the context of that model.

To his credit, like Aristotle and other earlier thinkers whose ideas he incorporated into his system, Ptolemy correctly postulated that the earth is a sphere. His logic for this insight was as follows:

> It is possible to see that the sun and moon and the other stars do not rise and set at the same time for every observer on the earth, but always earlier for those living towards the orient (i.e., the east) and later for those living towards the occident (i.e., the west). For we find that the phenomena of eclipses taking place at the same time, especially those of the moon, are not recorded at the same hours for everyone . . . but we always find later hours recorded for observers towards the orient than for those towards the occident. And since the differences in the hours is found to be proportional to the distances between the places, one would reasonably suppose the surface of the earth [to be] spherical, with the result that the general uniformity of curvature would assure every part's covering those following it proportionally.[91]

This, however, was one of the few key astronomical concepts that Ptolemy got right. In his scheme, the spherical earth rests, more or less unmoving, at the center of the heavens, an erroneous conclusion that he, like so many others before him, based on mere visual appearances. Since all bodies and weights fall toward the center of the earth, he reasoned, the earth must be in the center; and besides, if the earth did move, either in a straight line or around its own axis (rotation), people, animals, and other objects would float away. He wrote in Book I of the *Almagest*,

It is clear from the very appearances that the earth is in the middle of the world [i.e., the universe] and all weights move towards it. And the easiest and only way to understand this is to see that, once the earth has been proved spherical . . . and in the middle of the universe as we have said, then the tendencies and movements of heavy bodies . . . are everywhere and always at right angles to the tangent plane drawn through the falling body's point of contact with the earth's surface. For because of this it is clear that, if they were not stopped by the earth's surface, they too would go all the way to the center itself. . . . The solid body of the earth is reasonably considered as being the largest relative to those moving against it and as remaining unmoved in any direction by the force of the very small

An artist's conception of Ptolemy at work at the Alexandrian Museum's observatory. The device to the right is not a telescope, but a hollow tube used for observing individual stars or sky regions.

weights, and as it were absorbing their fall. And if it had some one common movement, the same as that of the other weights, it would clearly leave them all behind because of its much greater magnitude. And animals and other weights would be left hanging in the air, and the earth would very quickly fall out of the heavens. Merely to conceive such things makes them appear ridiculous.[92]

The Order Beneath the Disorder

Once he had established that the earth was an unmoving object resting at the center of the cosmos, Ptolemy went on, in page after page of detailed and ingenious mathematical diagrams and proofs, to explain how the heavenly bodies moved around the earth. Like other ancient astronomers, he accepted that their orbits were circular. But here again, he made a fundamental error. Not only do these bodies revolve around the sun, rather than the earth, but their orbits are elliptical (oval), not circular. From a modern viewpoint, it might seem odd that he and other Greek scientists so dogmatically insisted on the concept of circularity; but we must remember that it was difficult for them to conceive that the underlying structure of the heavens was not perfect and ordered; and the circle was seen as the most perfect and ordered geometrical form. "In Ptolemy's case," David Lindberg explains,

> the requirement of uniform circular motion was justified above all by the nature of the inquiry; his goal was not simply to set forth the relevant observational data, in order to describe the planetary motions in all of their complexity, but to reduce the complex planetary motions to their simplest components—to discover the real order underlying apparent disorder. And the simplest motion, representing the ultimate order, is, of course, uniform circular motion.[93]

The problem was that placing the sun, moon, planets, and stars in simple, straightforward circular orbits around the earth explained or accounted for only some of their observed motions. Since the beginning of recorded history, and likely long before, sky observers had noticed that all the planets occasionally slow down, stop, move backwards for a while, and then finally regain their "normal" forward (east to west) motion. This phenomenon is known as planetary "retrograde motion." Modern astronomy has shown that it results from the planets moving in their orbits at different velocities, so that sometimes a faster one "laps" a slower one, creating the visual illusion that the slower one moves backwards. A familiar analogy is the apparent backward movement of a car as seen from another car that passes it on the highway.

The true test, therefore, for Ptolemy's or anyone else's cosmic model was to explain satisfactorily the peculiarities of retrograde motion. He did so by elaborating on and perfecting an idea first tinkered with by the Greek astronomers Apollonius of Perga, circa 220 B.C., and Hipparchus, about 150 B.C., namely that of circular mathematical constructs called epicycles and deferents. American astronomer Thomas Arny offers this convenient summary of the way Ptolemy used these constructs in his own cosmic model:

> Ptolemy fashioned a model of planetary motions in which each planet moved on one small circle, which in turn moved on a larger one. The small circle, called an epicycle, was supposed to be carried along on the large circle [the deferent] like a Frisbee spinning on the rim of a bicycle wheel. According to Ptolemy's model, the motion of the planet from east to west across the night sky is caused by the rotation of the large circle (the bicycle wheel in our analogy). Retrograde motion occurs when the epicycle carries the planet in a reverse direction (caused by the rotation of the Frisbee in our model). Thus, with epicycles, it is possible to account for retrograde motion, and Ptolemy's model was able to predict planetary motions with fair precision.[94]

This fanciful European conception of Ptolemy shows him wearing clothes some twelve hundred years out of date.

Of course, Ptolemy's epicycles and deferents turned out to be nothing but an elaborate and very convincing illusion, as demonstrated by Copernicus, who proved once and for all that the sun resides at the center of the solar system.[95] Nevertheless, the Ptolemaic system, though wrong, was so well constructed that it remained enshrined in learned circles throughout medieval times. And the *Almagest*'s catalogue of the latitudes, longitudes, and magnitudes (degrees of brightness) of 1,022 stars in

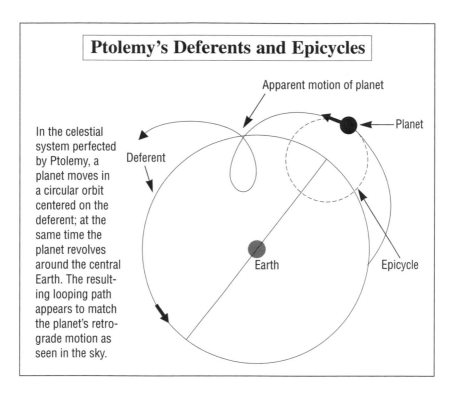

Ptolemy's Deferents and Epicycles

Apparent motion of planet

Planet

In the celestial system perfected by Ptolemy, a planet moves in a circular orbit centered on the deferent; at the same time the planet revolves around the central Earth. The resulting looping path appears to match the planet's retrograde motion as seen in the sky.

Deferent

Earth

Epicycle

forty-eight constellations continued as the standard reference work for sky maps in both the Western and Islamic worlds until the seventeenth century.

One of a Series of Investigators

Exactly when Ptolemy composed the *Almagest* is uncertain. But a few passing comments in the work itself offer clues. In Book IV, while describing some of his own celestial observations, he mentions an eclipse "observed in Alexandria in the year 9 Hadrian . . . at 3⅚ equatorial hours before midnight." [96] The term "9 Hadrian" means the ninth year of the reign of the Roman emperor Hadrian. Because Hadrian ascended the throne in the month and year corresponding to August A.D. 117 on our calendar, Ptolemy must have made this observation, the earliest listed in his masterwork, early in the year 127. The latest personal observation listed in the *Almagest* appears in Book X in a reference to "14 Antonine," or the fourteenth year of Antoninus Pius's reign, corresponding to late 151 or early 152. Therefore, it is likely that the observations used in compiling the work were made between 127 and 152. Of course, Ptolemy may not have finished writing the text itself until much later.

Ptolemy died about A.D. 178 having almost attained the age of eighty. The manner of his death, like most other personal information about him, is unknown. Had he some way of seeing into the future, he probably would have been surprised and dismayed to learn how astronomical research largely declined in the centuries immediately following his passing. In his view, one with which all modern scientists would readily concur, he was merely one of a series of investigators into nature's mysteries. His job, as he stated it in the introduction to the *Almagest,* was to examine the accumulated wisdom of his predecessors, add to and improve on their work as best as he could, and thereby pave the way for his successors, who would surely surpass him. "We ourselves," he wrote,

> try to increase continuously our love of the discipline of things which are always what they are [i.e., the unchanging laws of nature], by learning what has already been discovered in such sciences by those really applying themselves to them, and also by making a small original contribution such as the period of time from them to us could well make possible.[97]

In this respect, regardless of the ultimate rightness or wrongness of his various theories and conclusions, Ptolemy performed his job as a scientist exceedingly well.

CHAPTER 8

Galen: The Culmination of Ancient Medicine

Galen, a Greek physician who lived and worked in the second century A.D., the same period in which Ptolemy produced his geographical and astronomical writings, became the foremost medical practitioner of the Roman Empire. A brilliant, talented, and thoughtful scholar, Galen collected, analyzed, and utilized the work of the best doctors of the past. In particular, he admired and followed the precepts and methods of Hippocrates, the fifth-century B.C. Greek physician later dubbed the father of medicine. The most important contribution made by Hippocrates, his students, and the majority of his successors was to separate medical theory from religion, advocating, for example, that disease is not a divine punishment, but rather a natural phenomenon governed by natural laws.

Galen inherited and kept alive this impressive Greek medical tradition. One of his principal modern translators, Arthur Brock, states: "Galen's merit is to have crystallized or brought to a focus all the best work of the Greek medical schools which had preceded his own time." [98] In addition, through his own experiments, especially his dissections of dogs, pigs, and other animals, Galen added many new medical insights; and his hundreds of writings (eighty or so of which have survived) constitute the most comprehensive compilation of medical theory and practice produced in antiquity. David Lindberg writes,

> Galen addressed all the major medical issues of the day. He could be both practical, as in his pharmacology [description of medicinal drugs], and theoretical, as in his physiology [description of physical processes]. . . . His work . . . contained an impressive account of human anatomy and a brilliant synthesis of Greek psychological thought. In short, Galen offered a complete medical philosophy, which made excellent sense of the phenomena of health, disease, and healing. [99]

A late European painting fancifully depicts Hippocrates and Galen, the two greatest physicians of ancient times. Galen used the earlier healer's work as a basis for his own studies.

Considering that no Greek or Roman physician after Galen was able to match, let alone surpass, his knowledge and achievements, it is no wonder that he had a profound impact on later European scholars. Educated people in the Middle Ages and Renaissance held him in awe and he remained one of the two preeminent physicians of history (along with Hippocrates) until the dawn of the modern sciences of anatomy and physiology in the sixteenth and seventeenth centuries. Galen's work, then, marked the culmination of ancient medicine.

An Inquisitive Mind

Galen, whose name, quite appropriately it turned out, meant "gentle" or "peaceful," was born about A.D. 130 at Pergamum, a Greek city on the western coast of Asia Minor. The circumstances of his early childhood were unusually fortunate for two reasons. First, Pergamum was a prosperous and intellectually and politically enlightened city with a rich and diverse cultural life. Its library, housing some two hundred thousand works, was at the time the second largest in the ancient world, next to the great library adjoining the Museum in Alexandria; and Pergamum also boasted a spectacular shrine to the Greek healing god, Asclepius. For these reasons, the city regularly attracted philosophers, medical researchers, and other scholars and pilgrims from all over the Mediterranean world. Possessing an unusually bright and inquisitive mind, the young Galen could not help but be inspired and shaped by this fertile intellectual atmosphere.

Encouraged to Love Learning

Galen was also fortunate to come from a wealthy family that stressed the importance of education and could afford to hire the best tutors. Moreover, his father, Nicon, an engineer or architect by trade, was himself a dedicated scholar interested in a wide range of subjects, including mathematics, philosophy, literature, and the arts. Nicon encouraged his son to study these same subjects and overall to love learning and to be a discerning, highly critical thinker interested only in speaking and seeking the truth, important intellectual tools for any scientist. "I had the great good fortune to have a father who was extremely slow to anger, as well as extremely just, decent, and generous," Galen later wrote,

> and this awoke in me feelings of warmth and love for [my father]. . . . These, then . . . were the precepts I took from my father; and I keep them to this day. I do not declare allegiance to any sect, rather subjecting them all to a thorough examination; and I remain calm in the face of all events that may befall me from day to day—the same quality that I observed in my father. . . . Under my father's training I developed the habit of scorn for honor and reputation, and of respect for truth alone. I observe the grief that most people undergo at any perceived slight to their status, or at any financial loss. . . . I personally have never been observed to grieve for such losses. . . . I [have] always in mind the precept of my father, that one should not be troubled by any material loss provided that what remains is adequate for the care of one's body.[100]

Thanks in no small measure to his father's guidance, by the time Galen was seventeen he was a mature, level-headed young scholar thoroughly familiar with the works and ideas of Plato, Aristotle, and other important Greek thinkers. At about this time Nicon urged his son to begin specializing in medicine; and Galen became a pupil of Satyros, an eminent anatomist who lived and worked in Pergamum.

Less than a year later Nicon died unexpectedly and his son, who must have been devastated by the loss, decided to leave Pergamum. Galen journeyed first to the nearby city of Smyrna and studied for a while with a well-known doctor named Pelops; then the young man traveled widely in search of new medical knowledge, visiting Crete, Cyprus, Phoenicia, Palestine, and finally the greatest center of learning at the time—Alexandria. At the Alexandrian Museum and great library, Galen had firsthand access to all the writings of the leading medical researchers of the past, including the anatomists Herophilus and Erasistratus. Over time, Galen would enlarge on and surpass them, as, for example, in his frequent direct observations of various stages of digestion. On why food and fluids sometimes linger in the stomach, he correctly theorized that

Galen, picured here in later European garb, traveled extensively in his youth, visiting many Mediterranean cities, including Alexandria.

the actual cause of this is not, as one would imagine, that the lower outlet of the stomach, being fairly narrow, will allow nothing to pass before being reduced to a fine state of division. There are a great many people who frequently swallow large quantities of big fruit-stones; one person, who was holding a gold ring in his mouth, inadvertently swallowed it; another swallowed a coin . . . yet all these people easily passed by the bowel what they had swallowed, without there being any subsequent symptoms. Now surely if narrowness of the gastric outlet were the cause of undigested food remaining for an abnormally long time, none of these articles I have mentioned would ever have escaped.[101]

The Wonder-Worker

Around 157–158, now a highly competent physician in his late twenties, Galen returned to his native town of Pergamum. There he worked as a surgeon to gladiators, tending to the often gruesome wounds they received in combat. No doubt he did so partly to take advantage of one of the few legal ways of studying the human body's inner workings, since at the time dissecting people was forbidden by law. Galen also opened a private practice in Pergamum and began writing medical treatises. This stage of his career lasted only about four years, for about 161–162 he left home again, this time for Rome, then the capital and cultural hub of the Mediterranean world.

In Rome, Galen saw firsthand and was appalled by the lack of education, incompetence, and outright laziness displayed by many Roman doctors, including those who catered to the rich and famous. "Doctors will pay lip service to Hippocrates," he wrote,

> and look up to him as to a man without peer; but when it comes to taking the necessary steps to reach the same rank themselves—well, they do quite the opposite. . . . These people are not only personally ignorant [of nonmedical philosophy and science] . . . they actually censure others who are not equally ignorant. Furthermore, Hippocrates set great store by accurate knowledge of the body, as the starting point for the whole science of medicine; these doctors fail, in their studies, to learn [about] . . . each part of the body. . . . Do [today's doctors] lack the potential and

For a few years, Galen tended to the wounds of the gladiators who fought in the sports arena at Pergamum. This work taught him a great deal about human anatomy.

sufficient eagerness in their preparation for the art? . . . It must be because of the bad upbringing current in our times, and because of the higher value accorded to wealth as opposed to virtue, that we no longer get anyone of the quality of . . . Hippocrates among our doctors.[102]

Because his own skills as a physician and medical writer were so obviously superior to those of his colleagues, Galen's reputation steadily grew and his private practice and lectures attracted many wealthy and powerful Romans. One of these was the high government official Flavius Boethus, who introduced him to some of the leading political figures of the day, probably including the then reigning emperor, Marcus Aurelius. Galen soon became known in upper-class Roman circles as Paradoxologus, the "wonder-speaker," and Paradoxopoeus, the "wonder-worker." Many passages from his writings clearly reveal why he was so highly esteemed. This one, from *The Pulse for Beginners,* shows his keen powers of observation and his diligent efforts to refine his ability to make detailed diagnoses of his patients' symptoms:

> Exercise to begin with—and so long as it is practiced in moderation—renders the pulse vigorous, large, quick, and frequent. In cases of great excess, whereby the subject is scarcely still able to move . . . and there is a considerable loss of power, the pulse becomes very small, faint, slow, and sparse. . . . Hot baths, so long as they are kept in proportion, make the pulse large, quick, frequent, and vigorous. If they exceed this proportion, it becomes small and faint, though still fast and frequent. If continued in this state, they make it small, slow, sparse, and faint. The immediate effect of cold baths is to make the pulse small, slow, sparse, and rather faint.[103]

Personal Physician to the Emperors

Despite his popularity among well-to-do Romans, Galen's constant and harsh criticisms of his fellow doctors caused a great deal of controversy and bitter feelings; and perhaps to escape an increasingly stressful situation, early in the year 168 he left Rome and returned to his home in Pergamum. This attempted retirement was short-lived, however. As he himself told it:

> I returned from Rome to my native city after the completion of my thirty-seventh year . . . and was minding my own business; but there immediately arrived from Aquileia

Galen teaches an anatomy class in Rome. He was one of the last ancient scholars to conduct his own experiments and thereby to contribute to the advancement of knowledge.

> [in northeastern Italy] a summons under the imperial seal. The emperors had decided to attack the Germans in winter [and wanted Galen to accompany and attend to them during the campaign]. So I was forced to travel. I had hopes, though, of being excused: for I had heard that the older of the two emperors [Marcus Aurelius] was a reasonable man, understanding, gentle, and kind.[104]

Galen reluctantly made the journey and had no sooner reached Italy when he found his services sorely in need. "On my arrival in Aquileia," he recorded,

> there was an outbreak of the plague which caused destruction on a scale previously unknown. The emperors immediately fled to Rome with a small force of men; for the rest of us, survival became very difficult over a long period. The majority, in fact, died, the effects of the plague being compounded by the fact that all of this was taking place in the winter.[105]

Fortunately for Galen, his hopes of being excused from the military campaign were fulfilled. When Marcus Aurelius marched northward to fight the Germans, he left Galen in the post of personal physician to his son, the future emperor Commodus. Galen remained in Rome for the rest of his life, where he attended not only Aurelius and Commodus but also their three successors, the last being the gruff but capable former army general, Septimius Severus (reigned 193–211). Little is known about this final period of Galen's life, except that in it he produced a great many more medical writings and died about the year 200.

Galen on Christians and Slaves

These writings are very valuable to modern historians, not only for their documentation of the Greek and Roman medical knowledge of that era, but also for their descriptions of various social and religious groups. For instance, Galen was one of the few popular writers of his time who offered any detailed insights into the beliefs and practices of the early Christians, then still distrusted or hated by most Romans as antisocial or dangerous fanatics. The intelligent and gentle Galen was tolerant of the Christians, but viewed some of their beliefs as wrongheaded and silly. His comments about an idea that, as far as he knew, both Christians and Jews accepted—that God could have created men from stones if he had so desired—are revealing. They show how Galen and other Greek scientists tried to separate what they saw as rational theories and facts supported by evidence from irrational, unsupported superstitions.

> It is precisely this point in which our own opinion and that of Plato and the other Greeks who follow the right method in the natural sciences differ from the position taken up by Moses [i.e., in the Old Testament and other Judeo-Christian writings]. For the latter it seems enough to say that God simply willed the arrangement of matter and it was presently arranged in due order; for he believes everything to be possible with God, even should he wish to make a bull or a horse out of ashes. We, however, do not hold this [view]; we say that certain things are impossible by nature and that God does not even attempt such things at all.[106]

As an example, Galen offers human eyelashes, saying that their length and number are determined by what is best from a practical, and therefore natural, sense rather than by a divine mover arbitrarily willing them into existence. Similarly, he says, hair does not grow continuously from people's foreheads (as it does from the top of the head) for the practical reason that if it did it would obscure the vision.

Galen's writings are also an important source of information about the lives and experiences of members of the lower classes, whom most other ancient writers largely neglected in favor of the rich, powerful, and famous. The following well-known passage, for example, is one of his several documentations of the abuse of servants and slaves.

> Never did I lay hand upon a servant—a discipline practiced by my father too, who frequently berated friends who had bruised their hands in the act of hitting servants in the teeth. He would say that they [the masters] deserved to suffer convulsions and die from the inflammations they had sustained. . . . Once I even saw a man lose his temper and strike his servant in the eye with a reed-pen. And it is related of the emperor Hadrian [reigned 117–138] that he once struck one of his household staff in the eye with a pencil, causing

Roman slaves await the auction block. Galen regularly observed the way Roman masters treated their slaves, and his literary descriptions provide valuable information about the Roman slavery institution.

him to lose the sight of one eye. When Hadrian realized what had happened, he summoned the servant and agreed to grant him a gift of his own request in exchange for the loss he had suffered. But the injured party was silent. Hadrian repeated his offer: that he [the servant] should request anything he wished. At which the servant grew bold and said that he wanted nothing but his eye back. For what gift could compensate for the loss of an eye? [107]

The Unending Quest for the Truth

Not surprisingly, the scholars of the generations that immediately followed Galen's were far more interested in his medical observations than his social commentary. And in this respect it is ironic that he and his work contributed, quite inadvertently of course, to a steady decline in medical science in succeeding centuries. He was so skilled a doctor, researcher, observer, and writer that later Greek, Roman, and medieval European physicians regarded him as an unchallengeable authority, in a very real sense the last word in medicine. So they saw no need to carry on investigations of their own and medical experimentation largely ceased for over a thousand years.

These worshipers of Galen should have paid closer attention to what he himself had written in his work titled *The Best Doctor Is Also a Philosopher,* a gem of wisdom that sums up his whole approach to the study of medicine and to knowledge in general:

Galen was held in awe by later European scholars. Most studied and quoted his ideas instead of performing their own experiments.

The fact that we were born later than the ancients, and have inherited from them arts which they developed to such a high degree, should have been a considerable advantage. It would be easy, for example, to learn thoroughly in a very few years what Hippocrates discovered over a very long period of time, and then to devote the rest of one's life to the discovery of what remains. . . . There is nothing to prevent us, not only from reaching a similar attainment, but even from becoming better than him. For it is open to us to learn everything which he gave us a good account of, and then to find out the rest for ourselves.[108]

Indeed, the burning desire to discover "what remains" to be known about nature's mysteries was the guiding force that motivated ancient Greek scientists like Galen, Democritus, and Archimedes. In the fullness of time, new generations of scientists rediscovered that desire and went on to prove the existence of atoms and germs, to invent the telescope and vaccines, to harness the powers of steam, electricity, and other natural elements, and in general to transform the world. If for nothing else than their creation of the fundamental philosophy of true science—the unending quest for the truth—we and all of our descendants owe the Greeks a debt that can never be repaid.

NOTES

Chapter 1: A Brief History of Greek Science

1. George W. Botsford and Charles A. Robinson, *Hellenic History*. New York: Macmillan, 1956, pp. 97–98.

2. Rex Warner, *The Greek Philosophers*. New York: New American Library, 1958, pp. 9–10.

3. Homer, *Iliad*, from Book 17, "The Fight over Patroclus's Body." Translated by Don Nardo. Worthwhile translations of the complete work include those of W. H. D. Rouse (New York: New American Library, 1950), E. V. Rieu (Baltimore: Penguin Books, 1950), Richmond Lattimore (Chicago: University of Chicago Press, 1951), and Michael Reck (New York: HarperCollins, 1994).

4. Aristotle, *Metaphysics* and *On the Heavens*, quoted in Philip Wheelwright, ed., *The Presocratics*. New York: Macmillan, 1966, pp. 46–47.

5. Hippolytus, *Refutation of All Heresies*, quoted in Wheelwright, *The Presocratics*, p. 58.

6. A later Greek thinker, Empedocles, who lived and worked in the fifth century B.C. in the Greek town of Agrigentum on the island of Sicily, elaborated on Anaximander's theory of living things by speculating that at one time many different and varied species had existed. Some of these, Empedocles held, were ill-adapted to survive in the harsh conditions of their surroundings, so they died out, while stronger, more adaptable species took their place. Astoundingly, without the benefit of the immense wealth of factual data about plants and animals at Darwin's disposal, Empedocles had hit upon the kernel of the idea of natural selection, or "survival of the fittest."

7. From fragments of Anaxagoras's lost works, quoted in Wheelwright, *The Presocratics*, pp. 160–61.

8. It is likely that the Pythagorean idea of a spherical earth derived not only from the abstract and subjective notion that a sphere is "perfect," but also from direct observation. It was a well-known fact even then that as a distant ship approaches the shore one first sees the top of its masts and then, progressively, the rest of the vessel, a phenomenon that strongly suggests that the earth's surface is curved.

9. Quoted in Morris R. Cohen and I. E. Drabkin, *A Source Book in Greek Science.* Cambridge, MA: Harvard University Press, 1948, p. 96.

10. George Sarton, *A History of Science: Ancient Science Through the Golden Age of Greece.* Cambridge, MA: Harvard University Press, 1952, p. 289.

11. Warner, *The Greek Philosophers,* pp. 54–55.

12. Other scholars suggested alternative views that were closer to the truth, among them Heraclides of Pontus, who, in the 370s B.C., suggested that the earth rotates daily on its axis, and Aristarchus of Samos, born circa 310 B.C., the first known proponent of the heliocentric, or sun-centered, cosmic model; but these views, though now known to be correct, were not in the scientific mainstream of that time; as science historian David Lindberg points out, "Putting the earth in motion and giving it planetary status violated ancient authority, common sense, religious belief, and Aristotelian physics. . . . Whatever observational advantages it might have (for example, its ability to explain variations in the brightness of the planets) were available in other systems that did no violence to traditional cosmology." (*The Beginnings of Western Science.* Chicago: University of Chicago Press, 1992, p. 57.)

13. The inclusion of a prohibition against sexual abuse by physicians suggests that such abuses were known and that the medical establishment frowned on them.

14. Robert B. Downs, *Landmarks in Science: Hippocrates to Carson.* Littleton, CO: Libraries Unlimited, 1982, p. 22.

15. Pappus, *Mathematical Collection,* quoted in Cohen and Drabkin, *Source Book,* p. 184.

16. Vitruvius, *On Architecture,* vol. 10, quoted in L. Sprague de Camp, *The Ancient Engineers.* New York: Ballantine Books, 1963, p. 142. Reading this account naturally raises the question of why ancient inventors and machinists did not use such knowledge to develop more elaborate work-saving devices like those of the industrial revolution of the eighteenth and nineteenth centuries. The answer appears to be twofold. First, ancient metal-working techniques were incapable of producing cylinders and pistons of sufficient strength and accuracy. This placed a limit on the size and efficiency of machines using the principle, no matter how brilliant the inventor and his design. Second, the wealthy ruling classes felt no need or desire to in-

vest their money in work-saving machines. Perhaps this was because much cheaper labor, mostly in the form of slaves, was readily available.

17. Marshall Claggett, *Greek Science in Antiquity*. London: Abelard-Schuman, 1957, p. 182.

Chapter 2: Democritus: The First Atomic World View

18. Giorgio de Santillana, *The Origins of Scientific Thought, from Anaximander to Proclus, 600 B.C. to A.D. 300*. Chicago: University of Chicago Press, 1961, pp. 141–42.

19. Benjamin Farrington, *Science in Antiquity*. London: Oxford University Press, 1969, p. 46.

20. *Lives of the Eminent Philosophers,* quoted in Wheelwright, *The Presocratics*, p. 193.

21. From fragments of Democritus's works, quoted in Wheelwright, *The Presocratics*, p. 186.

22. From fragments of Democritus's works, quoted in Wheelwright, *The Presocratics*, p. 186.

23. Early versions of the atomic theory were advanced by members of India's Nyaya and Vaiseshika philosophy schools perhaps shortly after the birth of Christ. Democritus, visiting India over four centuries before, may have heard more primitive speculations about atomism by their predecessors. Even if this was the case, however, the idea had already been considered, completely independently, in Greece by Leucippus. For a fuller discussion, see Sarton, *History of Science*, pp. 254–55.

24. Simplicius, *Commentary on Aristotle's "On the Heavens,"* quoted in Cyril Bailey, *The Greek Atomists and Epicurus*. New York: Russell and Russell, 1964, p. 136.

25. From fragments of Democritus's works, quoted in Wheelwright, *The Presocratics*, p. 183.

26. Quoted in Wheelwright, *The Presocratics*, pp. 197–98.

27. Aristotle, *On Respiration*, quoted in Wheelwright, *The Presocratics*, p. 189.

28. Farrington, *Science in Antiquity*, p. 47.

29. *Lives*, quoted in Wheelwright, *The Presocratics*, p. 194.

30. From fragments of Democritus's works, quoted in Wheelwright, *The Presocratics*, pp. 185–86.

31. *Lives*, quoted in Wheelwright, *The Presocratics*, p. 196.

32. From fragments of Democritus's works, quoted in Santillana, *Origins of Scientific Thought,* p. 142.

Chapter 3: Plato: The Creation of the Universe

33. The war's name derived from the Peloponnesus, the large peninsula that makes up the southern third of Greece and where Sparta and many of its allies were located.

34. Plato, *Gorgias,* translated by Benjamin Jowett, in *Great Books of the Western World,* vol. 7. Chicago: Encyclopaedia Britannica, 1952, p. 290. In the dialogue, written when Plato was about forty, these words are spoken by Socrates, whom Plato used as a central character in most of his dialogues.

35. Robert B. Downs, *Books That Changed the World.* New York: Penguin Books, 1983, pp. 57, 59–60.

36. Nickolas Pappas, *Plato and the Republic.* London: Routledge, 1995, pp. 5–6.

37. The real reasons behind his elimination are somewhat unclear, but foremost among them were probably his frequent criticism of Athenian democracy and the fact that Alcibiades, a statesman who had turned traitor during the great war and caused the death of thousands of Athenian soldiers, and Critias, the chief member of a group of tyrants who imposed a reign of terror on Athens in the months following its defeat, were both former friends and followers of Socrates. For a concise but thorough overview of the background, events, and impact of the trial, see Don Nardo, *The Trial of Socrates.* San Diego: Lucent Books, 1997.

38. Plato, *Seventh Letter,* translated by J. Harwood, in *Great Books,* vol. 7, pp. 800–801. It should be noted that some modern scholars have expressed doubts about the authenticity of the events described in the letter; one view is that Plato did not write it, while another suggests that he wrote it but purposely slanted the events for political reasons.

39. Sarton, *History of Science,* p. 402.

40. *Timaeus* 28, in *Great Books,* vol. 7, p. 447.

41. *Timaeus* 28, in *Great Books,* vol. 7, p. 447.

42. Lindberg, *Beginnings of Western Science,* p. 40.

43. *Timaeus* 28, in *Great Books,* vol. 7, p. 447.

44. Plato's conception that the universe is constructed of perfect geometrical shapes whose movements adhere to unerring math-

ematical principles followed the traditional view of the Pythagoreans. However, he was repelled by most other pre-Socratic scientific notions, including atomism, finding their lack of a divine mover cold and materialistic. His conception of a Demiurge, who could reason and plan, was an attempt to impose on the cosmos what he viewed as a rational order.

45. Sarton, *History of Science,* pp. 420–21, 423.

Chapter 4: Aristotle: The Classification of Animals

46. Downs, *Landmarks of Science,* p. 25.

47. Renford Bambrough, *The Philosophy of Aristotle.* New York: New American Library, 1963, p. 11.

48. G. E. R. Lloyd, *Aristotle: The Growth and Structure of His Thought.* New York: Cambridge University Press, 1968, p. 314.

49. Louise R. Loomis, *Aristotle on Man and the Universe.* Roslyn, NY: Walter J. Black, 1943.

50. The explanation advanced by some scholars, that Aristotle left because he was upset that he himself did not become head of the school, is almost certainly wrong. The school and the property on which it sat had belonged to Plato. As a resident alien in Athens, Aristotle was, under the city's laws, barred from owning such property, which naturally passed on to a member of Plato's family.

51. In 338 B.C., Philip and Alexander defeated a coalition of Greek states led by Athens and Thebes, allowing Philip to impose his will on most of Greece.

52. A. E. Taylor, *Aristotle.* New York: Dover Publications, 1955, p. 12.

53. *On the Heavens,* quoted in Cohen and Drabkin, *Source Book,* p. 148.

54. *Metaphysics,* quoted in Cohen and Drabkin, *Source Book,* p. 103.

55. Theodore E. James, introduction to Thomas P. Kiernan, ed., *Aristotle Dictionary.* New York: Philosophical Library, 1962, p. 12.

56. He described and discussed some 540 species in all.

57. *History of Animals,* quoted in Cohen and Drabkin, *Source Book,* p. 422.

58. For example, maggots routinely appeared on decaying meat, mice in garbage, and insects in damp hay. In reality, of course, flies lay their eggs in meat, giving rise to maggots, mice are *attracted to* rather than *created in* garbage, and so on.

59. *History of Animals,* quoted in Sarton, *History of Science,* p. 534.

60. Sarton, *History of Science,* p. 544.

Chapter 5: Theophrastus: The Foundations of Botany

61. Sarton, *History of Science,* p. 558.

62. *Characters* 12, in Jeffrey Rusten, ed. and trans., *Theophrastus: Characters.* Cambridge, MA: Harvard University Press, 1993, pp. 97–99.

63. *Characters,* 16, in Rusten translation, pp. 107–13.

64. *History of Plants,* in Arthur Hort, trans., *Theophrastus: Inquiry into Plants and Minor Works on Odors and Weather Signs.* Cambridge, MA: Harvard University Press, 1961, pp. 311–13.

65. *History of Plants,* in Hort translation, pp. 105–107.

66. *History of Plants,* in Hort translation, p. 155.

67. As late as the 1600s, some leading herbalists referred to Theophrastus's description of hand-pollination as a fable.

68. Quoted in Sarton, *History of Science,* p. 560.

69. Quoted in Werner Jaeger, *Aristotle.* Oxford: Clarendon Press, 1948, p. 315.

Chapter 6: Archimedes: The Application of Mechanical Principles

70. Quoted in Cohen and Drabkin, *Source Book,* pp. 184–85.

71. *On the Sphere and Cylinder, On Conoids and Spheroids, On Spirals,* and *Quadrature of the Parabola* are all addressed to Dositheus; *The Method of Treating Mechanical Problems* is addressed to Eratosthenes.

72. Plutarch, *Life of Marcellus,* in *Plutarch: Makers of Rome.* Translated by Ian Scott-Kilvert. New York: Penguin Books, 1965, p. 102.

73. Plutarch, *Marcellus,* in *Makers,* p. 98.

74. The modern word "eureka" appears to have derived from a later copyist's error in which the "h" of the original Greek word was dropped.

75. Vitruvius, *On Architecture,* vol. 9, quoted in de Camp, *The Ancient Engineers,* pp. 155–56.

76. The principle also applies to bodies surrounded by gases and the air, as in the case of balloons, which, for instance, rise (or in technical terms are displaced upwards) when they are filled with a gas lighter than air.

77. *On the Equilibrium of Planes,* in Archimedes, *Works.* Translated by Thomas L. Heath, in *Great Books of the Western World,* vol. 11. Chicago: Encyclopaedia Britannica, 1952, p. 502.

78. Plutarch, *Marcellus,* in *Makers,* p. 99.

79. Quoted in Cohen and Drabkin, *Source Book,* pp. 142–43.

80. *Marcellus,* in *Makers,* p. 100. Plutarch devotes a fair amount of space to Archimedes' defensive weapons in an exciting, detailed account of the siege that is well worth the effort of reading in its entirety. See also the account by the second-century B.C. Greek historian Polybius (*The Histories.* Translated by W. R. Paton. Cambridge, MA: Harvard University Press, 1966, vol. 3, pp. 457–59).

81. *Marcellus,* in *Makers,* p. 101.

82. *Marcellus,* in *Makers,* p. 101.

83. *Marcellus,* in *Makers,* p. 104.

84. Lindberg, *Beginnings of Western Science,* p. 110.

Chapter 7: Ptolemy: The Mapping of the Earth and Heavens

85. Owen Gingerich, *The Eye of Heaven: Ptolemy, Copernicus, Kepler.* New York: American Institute of Physics, 1993, p. 5.

86. A few ancient sources claim that he was born much farther north, at Pelusium, on the Mediterranean seacoast east of the Nile delta.

87. The Greek Ptolemaic dynasty was founded in the late fourth century B.C. by Ptolemy I, who had been one of Alexander the Great's leading generals and successors and who took control of Egypt following Alexander's death. Ptolemy's descendants ruled Egypt until 31 B.C., when the last Ptolemaic ruler, Cleopatra VII, was defeated at Actium by Octavian (later Augustus, the first Roman emperor) and committed suicide. Soon afterward, Rome annexed Egypt as a province.

88. Quoted in Santillana, *Origins of Scientific Thought,* p. 274.

89. Quoted in Santillana, *Origins of Scientific Thought,* p. 274.

90. Downs, *Landmarks in Science,* p. 56.

91. *Almagest.* Translated by R. Catesby Taliaferro, in *Great Books of the Western World,* vol. 16. Chicago: Encyclopaedia Britannica, 1952, pp. 8–9.

92. *Almagest,* in *Great Books,* vol. 16, p. 11.

93. Lindberg, *Beginnings of Western Science,* p. 102.

94. Thomas T. Arny, *Explorations: An Introduction to Astronomy.* St. Louis: Mosby, 1994, p. 41.

95. For the text of Copernicus's revolutionary masterwork, see *On the Revolutions of the Heavenly Spheres.* Translated by Charles G. Wallace, in *Great Books of the Western World,* vol. 16. Chicago: Encyclopaedia Britannica, 1952. An informative and very well written modern secondary study of his life and work is Angus Armitage's *The World of Copernicus.* New York: New American Library, 1947.

96. *Almagest,* in *Great Books,* vol. 16, p. 136.

97. *Almagest,* in *Great Books,* vol. 16, p. 6.

Chapter 8: Galen: The Culmination of Ancient Medicine

98. Arthur J. Brock, introduction to Galen, *On the Natural Faculties.* Translated by Arthur J. Brock, in *Great Books of the Western World,* vol. 10. Chicago: Encyclopaedia Britannica, 1952, p. ix.

99. Lindberg, *Beginnings of Western Science,* pp. 129–30.

100. *The Affections and Errors of the Soul,* in *Galen: Selected Works.* Translated by P. N. Singer. New York: Oxford University Press, 1997, pp. 119–21. By contrast, Galen had nothing good to say about his mother, who, he claimed, "was so bad-tempered that she would sometimes bite her maids; she was perpetually shouting and fighting with my father" (p. 119).

101. *On the Natural Faculties,* in *Great Books,* vol. 10, p. 201.

102. *The Best Doctor Is Also a Philosopher,* in *Selected Works,* pp. 30–31.

103. In *Selected Works,* p. 332.

104. *My Own Books,* in *Selected Works,* pp. 7–8. Galen's reference to "two emperors" includes Lucius Verus, an aristocrat whom Marcus Aurelius appointed as co-emperor shortly after ascending the throne in 161; Verus fell ill and died in the spring of 168, on the very campaign Galen here describes.

105. *My Own Books,* in *Selected Works,* p. 8.

106. *On the Usefulness of the Parts of the Body,* quoted in Robert L. Wilken, *The Christians as the Romans Saw Them.* New Haven: Yale University Press, 1984, pp. 86–87.

107. *The Affections and Errors of the Soul,* in *Selected Works,* pp. 107–108.

108. In *Selected Works,* pp. 31–32, 34.

CHRONOLOGY

B.C.

ca. 600
The ancient Greeks begin to develop a systematic approach to the study of science.

ca. 575
Thales, a resident of the Greek city of Miletus, establishes the Ionian philosophical-scientific school; he proposes that nature's underlying physical substance is water.

ca. 530
Pythagoras and his followers establish another school of learning at Crotona, in southern Italy; the Pythagoreans suggest that numbers and mathematical relationships underlie nature's structure.

ca. 500–428
Life of Anaxagoras, who proposes that the "seeds" of everything are contained in all substances.

ca. 460–360
Life of Democritus, who refines and restates the atomic theory proposed by Leucippus a few decades earlier.

ca. 427–347
Life of Plato, who develops a comprehensive cosmology based partly on the ideas of the Pythagoreans.

ca. 407
Plato becomes a devoted follower of the Athenian philosopher Socrates.

399
Death of Socrates, whose "Socratic method" of inquiry will later be adapted to science by Plato, Aristotle, and others.

ca. 380s
Plato establishes the Athenian Academy, the first formal school of higher learning in ancient times.

384–322
Life of Aristotle, the most influential of all ancient philosopher-scientists.

ca. 370–285
Life of Theophrastus, later called the father of botany, who meets and befriends Aristotle at the Academy.

367
Aristotle enrolls at Plato's Academy, where he will remain for some twenty years.

347
Plato dies; Aristotle leaves the Academy and moves to Asia Minor.

335
Aristotle establishes his own school, the Lyceum, in Athens.

ca. 319
Theophrastus composes his work, the *Characters*.

ca. 287–212
Life of Archimedes, the greatest mathematician and inventor of ancient times, who studies at the Museum, the famous center for scientific studies adjoining the great library at Alexandria, Egypt.

ca. 284–192
Life of Eratosthenes, who, while working at the Museum, measures the circumference of the earth with amazing accuracy.

213–212
During the Roman siege of his native city of Syracuse, Archimedes employs huge, devastating defensive weapons that inflict serious casualties on the attackers.

A.D.
ca. 100–178
Life of Ptolemy, who writes a geographical atlas that will remain in use for over fourteen centuries, and whose treatise, the *Almagest*, marks the culmination of ancient astronomical theory.

ca. 127–152
Ptolemy makes the bulk of the celestial observations listed in his *Almagest*.

ca. 130–200
Life of Galen, the most important ancient Greek medical figure after Hippocrates (fifth century B.C.).

ca. 147–157
Galen travels around the Mediterranean world in search of medical knowledge, living and studying for a while in Alexandria.

168
Galen becomes personal physician to the family of the emperor Marcus Aurelius.

476
The last western Roman emperor vacates his throne; in the following few centuries, as the political, administrative, and cultural framework

of the Roman Empire steadily disintegrates, Greek and Roman learning, including science, rapidly declines.

ca. 1000

Arabic translations of the major ancient Greek scientific treatises, largely forgotten for centuries in Europe, begin to filter into European educated circles.

1543

Polish astronomer Nicolaus Copernicus publishes *On the Revolutions of the Heavenly Spheres,* which champions a sun-centered universe and proves wrong the long-accepted earth-centered cosmological worldview formulated by Plato, Aristotle, and Ptolemy.

FOR FURTHER READING

Kathlyn Gay, *Science in Ancient Greece*. New York: Franklin Watts, 1988. With a text aimed at basic readers (grades four through seven), this useful volume discusses the major figures of ancient Greek science, including Thales, Democritus, Aristotle, Hipparchus, and Hippocrates.

A. Rupert Hall and Marie B. Hall, *A Brief History of Science*. New York: New American Library, 1964. The first six chapters constitute an excellent overview of the trends and ideas of ancient and medieval science. Reading level is geared to high schoolers and up.

Carol Moss, *Science in Ancient Mesopotamia*. New York: Franklin Watts, 1988. Basic readers are here introduced to the major scientific contributions of the Sumerians and Babylonians in areas such as medicine, mathematics, astronomy, and building materials.

Don Nardo, *Gravity*. San Diego: Lucent Books, 1990. The first few chapters of this volume provide a concise overview of how the Copernican conception of the cosmos developed out of ancient and medieval conceptions.

———, *Ancient Greece*. San Diego: Lucent Books, 1994; *Life in Ancient Greece*. San Diego: Lucent Books, 1996. These concise but detailed overviews of Greek civilization provide a context for understanding Greek science by exploring the major political, cultural, and literary trends and events that surrounded and influenced the development of this science.

———, *Greek and Roman Science*. San Diego: Lucent Books, 1997. A comprehensive but easy-to-read volume that complements this one on the lives of Greek scientists by providing a broader overview of the development of Greek scientific thought and how it affected the very different Roman approach to science.

Colin Ronan, *Lost Discoveries: The Forgotten Science of the Ancient World*. New York: McGraw-Hill, 1973. A well-written and very handsomely illustrated presentation of some of the most important ancient scientific thinkers and their discoveries, including

Aristarchus, Aristotle, Eratosthenes, Theophrastus, Archimedes, and many others. Reading level is geared to ambitious junior high schoolers and up.

Geraldine Woods, *Science in Ancient Egypt.* New York: Franklin Watts, 1988. Mathematics, astronomy, timekeeping, medicine, crafts, technology, agriculture, and the building of the pyramids are among the topics covered in this overview of ancient Egyptian science for basic readers.

MAJOR WORKS CONSULTED

Morris R. Cohen and I. E. Drabkin, *A Source Book in Greek Science.* Cambridge, MA: Harvard University Press, 1948. This fulsome, comprehensive book is the standard modern source consulted by classical scholars for key excerpts from the writings of ancient Greek (and a few Roman) scientists. Includes translations of Aristotle, Plato, Theophrastus, Ptolemy, Hippocrates, Galen, Plutarch (on Archimedes), Vitruvius (on Greek inventions), and dozens of others.

L. Sprague de Camp, *The Ancient Engineers.* New York: Ballantine Books, 1963. This famous book, written in de Camp's always engaging style, remains a gold mine of useful and interesting information about how the ancients discovered and applied a host of scientific principles. Very highly recommended.

Robert B. Downs, *Landmarks in Science: Hippocrates to Carson.* Littleton, CO: Libraries Unlimited, 1982. Downs, a fine writer and author of the insightful and useful *Books That Changed the World* (New York: Penguin Books, 1983), here devotes a chapter each to Hippocrates, Aristotle, Theophrastus, Archimedes, Ptolemy, Galen, and other Greek scientists, and then goes on to do the same with later medieval and modern scientists.

Benjamin Farrington, *Science in Antiquity.* London: Oxford University Press, 1969. Farrington delivers a thoughtful, somewhat scholarly examination of the development of science from ancient Babylonia through the fall of Rome.

David C. Lindberg, *The Beginnings of Western Science.* Chicago: University of Chicago Press, 1992. A very well written overview of the development of science from early Greek to late medieval times. Highly recommended.

Stephen F. Mason, *A History of the Sciences.* New York: Collier Books, 1962. A commendable concise history, tracing discoveries of scientific principles from Babylonia and Egypt, through Greece, Rome, medieval Europe, the modern scientific revolution, and the twentieth century.

George Sarton, *A History of Science: Ancient Science Through the Golden Age of Greece.* Cambridge, MA: Harvard University Press, 1952. A Belgian-born Harvard University professor and scholar, Sarton (1884–1956) is widely recognized as the twentieth century's leading authority on the history of science. This comprehensive, detailed study of early Greek science is undoubtedly one of the masterworks in the field, although it will appeal mainly to scholars, teachers, and serious history buffs.

Rex Warner, *The Greek Philosophers*. New York: New American Library, 1958. A renowned scholar/translator here offers a well-written synopsis of the major Greek thinkers, from Thales and other pre-Socratics to Plotinus and others in the Roman period; features sample primary source materials for each person covered.

ADDITIONAL WORKS CONSULTED

Ancient Sources

Archimedes, *Works*. Translated by Thomas L. Heath, in *Great Books of the Western World,* vol. 11. Chicago: Encyclopaedia Britannica, 1952.

Aristotle, *Complete Works*. Translated by Robert M. Hutchins, in *Great Books of the Western World,* vols. 8 and 9. Chicago: Encyclopaedia Britannica, 1952; and assorted excerpts from Aristotle's works in Thomas P. Kiernan, ed., *Aristotle Dictionary.* New York: Philosophical Library, 1962.

Galen, *On the Natural Faculties*. Translated by Arthur J. Brock, in *Great Books of the Western World,* vol. 10. Chicago: Encyclopaedia Britannica, 1952; and various works in *Greek Medicine: Being Extracts Illustrative of Medical Writers from Hippocrates to Galen.* Translated by Arthur J. Brock. New York: E. P. Dutton, 1929; and various other works in *Galen: Selected Works.* Translated by P. N. Singer. New York: Oxford University Press, 1997.

Plato, *Dialogues*. Translated by Benjamin Jowett, in *Great Books of the Western World,* vol. 7. Chicago: Encyclopaedia Britannica, 1952. Jowett's translation is also available in New York: Random House, 1937, with various newer reprints. The most important dialogue from a scientific point of view is the *Timaeus.*

Plutarch, *Parallel Lives,* excerpted in *The Rise and Fall of Athens: Nine Greek Lives by Plutarch.* Translated by Ian Scott-Kilvert. New York: Penguin Books, 1960; and *Plutarch: Makers of Rome.* Translated by Ian Scott-Kilvert. New York: Penguin Books, 1965.

Ptolemy, *Almagest*. Translated by R. Catesby Taliaferro, in *Great Books of the Western World,* vol. 16. Chicago: Encyclopaedia Britannica, 1952.

Theophrastus, *Characters*. Translated by Jeffrey Rusten. Cambridge, MA: Harvard University Press, 1993; and *History of Plants,* in Arthur Hort, trans., *Theophrastus: Inquiry into Plants and Minor Works on Odors and Weather Signs.* Cambridge, MA: Harvard University Press, 1961.

Author's Note: In the cases of lesser known ancient authors or where I deem a translation of a major author clearer, I have taken primary source quotes from translations cited in secondary works, primarily Cohen and Drabkin's *Source Book of Greek Science,* Sarton's *History of Science,* Warner's *Greek Philosophers* (all three see Major Works Consulted), and Wheelwright's *The Presocratics* (see below).

Modern Sources

Angus Armitage, *The World of Copernicus* (original title: *Sun Stand Thou Still*). New York: New American Library, 1947.

Thomas T. Arny, *Explorations: An Introduction to Astronomy.* St. Louis: Mosby, 1994.

Cyril Bailey, *The Greek Atomists and Epicurus.* New York: Russell and Russell, 1964.

Renford Bambrough, *The Philosophy of Aristotle.* New York: New American Library, 1963.

George W. Botsford and Charles A. Robinson, *Hellenic History.* New York: Macmillan, 1956.

Marshall Claggett, *Greek Science in Antiquity.* London: Abelard-Schuman, 1957.

J. G. Crowther, *A Short History of Science.* London: Methuen, 1969.

Owen Gingerich, *The Eye of Heaven: Ptolemy, Copernicus, Kepler.* New York: American Institute of Physics, 1993.

Werner Jaeger, *Aristotle.* Oxford: Clarendon Press, 1948.

Rocky Kolb, *Blind Watchers of the Sky: The People and Ideas that Shaped Our View of the Universe.* Reading, MA: Addison-Wesley, 1996.

G. E. R. Lloyd, *Aristotle: The Growth and Structure of His Thought.* New York: Cambridge University Press, 1968.

Louise R. Loomis, *Aristotle on Man and the Universe.* Roslyn, NY: Walter J. Black, 1943.

John E. Murdoch, *Album of Science: Antiquity and the Middle Ages.* New York: Scribner's, 1984.

De Lacy O'Leary, *How Greek Science Passed to the Arabs.* London: Routledge and Kegan Paul, 1949.

Richard Olson, *Science Deified and Science Defied: The Historical Significance of Science in Western Culture from the Bronze Age to the Beginnings of the Modern Era ca. 3500 B.C. to ca. A.D. 1640.* Berkeley and Los Angeles: University of California Press, 1982.

Nickolas Pappas, *Plato and the Republic.* London: Routledge, 1995.

Arnold Reymond, *History of the Sciences in Greco-Roman Antiquity.* Translated by Ruth Gheury De Bray. New York: Biblo and Tannen, 1965.

Giorgio de Santillana, *The Origins of Scientific Thought, from Anaximander to Proclus, 600 B.C. to A.D. 300.* Chicago: University of Chicago Press, 1961.

Richard J. A. Talbert, ed., *Atlas of Classical History.* London: Routledge, 1985.

A. E. Taylor, *Aristotle.* New York: Dover Publications, 1955.

John Warry, *Warfare in the Classical World.* Norman: University of Oklahoma Press, 1995.

Eugen Weber, ed., *The Western Tradition, from the Ancient World to Louis XIV.* Boston: D. C. Heath, 1965.

Philip Wheelwright, ed., *The Presocratics.* New York: Macmillan, 1966.

Robert L. Wilken, *The Christians as the Romans Saw Them.* New Haven: Yale University Press, 1984.

INDEX

Picture Credits

Cover photos: Clockwise from top left: North Wind Picture Archives; North Wind Picture Archives; Corbis; Stock Montage, Inc.; Library of Congress; North Wind Picture Archives; Stock Montage, Inc.

Corbis, 95

Corbis-Bettmann, 13, 27, 32, 41, 59, 62, 72, 76, 97

Heck's Pictorial Archive of Art and Architecture, Dover Publications, 48

Heck's Pictorial Archive of Military Science, Geography and History, Dover Publications, 28

Hulton-Getty Picture Collection/Tony Stone Images, 60

Library of Congress, 12, 21, 22, 53, 55, 88, 42

North Wind Picture Archives, 9, 16, 18, 19, 24, 37, 40, 44, 46, 50, 69, 99, 100

Prints Old and Rare, 77, 82

Scala/Art Resource, NY, 35, 92

Stock Montage, Inc., 34, 57, 65, 66, 74, 80, 83, 86, 94

Baldwin H. Ward/Corbis-Bettmann, 30

ABOUT THE AUTHOR

Historian and award-winning writer Don Nardo has published more than twenty books about the ancient Greek and Roman world. These include general histories, such as *The Roman Empire, The Persian Empire,* and *Philip and Alexander: The Unification of Greece*; war chronicles, such as *The Punic Wars* and *The Battle of Marathon*; cultural studies, such as *Life in Ancient Greece, Greek and Roman Theater, The Age of Augustus,* and *The Trial of Socrates*; and literary companions to the works of Homer and Sophocles. Mr. Nardo also writes screenplays and teleplays and composes music. He lives with his wife, Christine, and dog, Bud, on Cape Cod, Massachusetts.